World of Music

CARMEN E. CULP • LAWRENCE EISMAN

MARY E. HOFFMAN

Authors

CARMINO RAVOSA

Theme Musical

DARRELL BLEDSOE

Producer, Vocal Recordings

PHYLLIS WEIKART

Rhythmic Movement

Silver Burdett & Ginn

Morristown, NJ • Needham, MA

Atlanta, GA • Cincinnati, OH • Dallas, TX • Menlo Park, CA • Deerfield, IL

CONTENTS

SECTION I MUSIC FOR LIVING 2

UNIT 1 Introduction: Beginnings 4

UNIT 2 A Blend of Two Worlds 8

UNIT 3 Style 24

UNIT 4 The Classic and Romantic Periods 38

UNIT 5 The Twentieth Century 54

UNIT 6 Singing in Groups 70

Fine Arts 39, 71, 81, 82
Meet the Composer
• Wolfgang Amadeus Mozart 37
• Dimitri Shostakovich 37
• Franz Liszt 52
• Johannes Brahms 53
Listening Library 4, 12–15, 17, 19, 20, 23, 25,
                        29, 33, 36, 51, 52, 56, 58–60,
                        62, 64, 66–70, 73, 82
Evaluations 86

SECTION II UNDERSTANDING MUSIC 92

UNIT 1 Melody 94

UNIT 2 Rhythm 116

UNIT 3 Harmony 130

UNIT 4 Tone Color 136

UNIT 5 Patterns into Form 142

Fine Arts 137, 167
Related Poetry 136
Meet the Composer
• Edvard Grieg 149
Listening Library 105, 110, 118, 124, 125, 129,
                      133, 136, 138–142, 144–147,
                      149, 150, 152, 155, 157, 160,
                      163, 164, 170, 173–175
Careers in Music 164
Evaluations 177

SECTION III MAKING MUSIC 182

UNIT 1 Performing in Ensembles 184

UNIT 2 Following a Score 200

UNIT 3 Theme Musical: Don't Go Anywhere
Without a Song 210

UNIT 4 Stage Musical: Oliver! 216

Listening Library 184, 186, 187, 189, 192–195,
197–199, 207, 208, 216, 219,
228, 233

Careers in Music 208
Evaluations 246

SECTION IV SING AND CELEBRATE 252

Song Unit 254–304

REFERENCE BANK

Learning to Play Guitar 306
Can You Read This? 320
The Sound Bank 324
Glossary 328
Classified Index 331
Song Index 333
Picture Credits 334

MUSIC FOR LIVING

Introduction: Beginnings

People make music in many ways. They may play instruments with others in bands, orchestras, jazz ensembles, and rock groups. Or, they may play by themselves on piano or organ, guitar or harmonica. Almost everyone can sing—from those who manage to belt out a tune in the shower to those who sing in folk groups, choirs, in opera houses, and in Broadway theaters. Some teach singing, or serve in churches and synagogues as choirmasters and cantors.

"Sing," on page 5, is all *about* singing. "Ja-Da," on page 6, is a lively song from the beginning of the jazz age. "Nine Hundred Miles," on page 7, is a work song from the black tradition. Learn to sing these songs. Sing for the joy of it. Just relax, enjoy, and SING . . .

Collage of Musical Performers

Sing

Words and Music by Joe Raposo

Guitar: capo 3

La la la la la, La la la la la la, La la la la la la la.___

(sing echo 2nd time)

Sing! Sing! Sing a song. Sing a song. Sing out loud. Sing out

loud. Sing out strong. Sing out strong. Sing of good things, not

bad. Sing of hap - py, not sad.

Sing! Sing! Sing a song. Sing a song. Make it

sim - ple to last your whole life long.___ Don't

wor - ry that it's not good e - nough, __ for an - y - one else to hear.

Sing! Sing a song!___

(Repeat and fade)

La la la la la, La la la la la la, La la la la la la la.___

Ja-Da

Words and Music by Bob Carleton

Guitar: capo 3

1. You've heard all a-bout your rag-gy mel-o-dy,_ Ev-'ry thing from op-'ra down to
2. Our bands have been dig-ging back for tunes to be sung,_ Op-er-as and nurs-'ry rhymes have

har-mo-ny,_ But I've a lit-tle song that I will sing to you,_ It's
been o-ver-done,_ I dug a lit-tle deep-er and I found this thing,_ It's

gon-na win you through and through.__ There's not much to the words but the
rag-time, but it still can swing.___ It's not a tur-key trot or a

mu-sic is grand,_ And you'll be a-sing-ing it to beat _ the band._ You've
shim-my one-step,_ But when grand-ma danced to it, she thought she was hep,_ It

heard of the tis-ket and tas-ket, it's true,_ But give a lit-tle lis-ten to this,_
still is a dit-ty, I'm sure you will find,_ Will keep a run-nin' 'round and a-round_

REFRAIN

_ will you?_ Ja - Da,___ Ja - Da,___
_ your mind._

Ja - Da, Ja - Da, Jing, Jing, Jing, ___ Ja - Da, ___ Ja - Da,

Ja - Da, Ja - Da, Jing, Jing, Jing, ___ That's a fun-ny lit-tle bit of mel - o - dy ___ It's so sooth -ing and ap - peal-ing to me, ___ It goes

Ja - Da, ___ Ja - Da, ___ Ja - Da, Ja - Da, Jing, Jing, Jing. ___

Nine Hundred Miles

African-American Work Song   Arranged and Adapted by Cisco Houston

1. I am rid - in' on this train, There are tears in ___ my eyes.
     train ___ I ride on Is a hundred coach - es long. You can
     pawn ___ you my watch And I'll pawn you ___ my chain. I'll ___

Tryin' to read a let - ter from my home. ___ If this train runs me
hear the whis -tle blow a hun-dred miles. ___ And the lonesome whis -tle
pawn ___ you my gold ___ dia-mond ring. ___ For if this train runs me

right, I'll be home Sat -ur-day night, For I'm nine hun-dred miles from ___ my
call is the mournful -est ___ of all, 'Cause it's nine hun-dred miles from ___ my
right, I'll be home Sat -ur-day night, For I'm nine hun-dred miles from ___ my

1., 2.

home. ___

3.

home. ___
home. ___

          2. Well, this
          3. Well, I'll   home. ___

The Slave Routes

British Colonies
Boston
New York
Philadelphia
Norfolk
Charles Town
New Orleans
Cuba
Jamaica
Hispaniola
Porto Rico

England
France
Portugal
Spain

Africa
Cape Castle
São Paulo de Locanda

Peru
Brazil
Bahia
São Paulo
Rio de Janeiro

A TRIP TO ANOTHER WORLD

Imagine! Your community is kidnapped by aliens from outer space. The people are taken to work as slaves in a galaxy far, far away!

Sound unbelievable? Something like that happened to millions of people who lived in western and central Africa from the sixteenth through the nineteenth centuries. Rival groups sometimes captured their weaker neighbors and sold them to European and American sea captains. These sea captains took the captives to North and South America to be sold into slavery.

Some countries—for example, Brazil—and the Spanish and French islands in the Caribbean allowed the slaves to retain their old-world customs, and so their music changed very little. Other countries, however, including the United States, would not allow slaves to practice their traditions. Even their music was forbidden. The slave owners in these countries were afraid that Africans would use their language and music to communicate secretly. The slave owners were right! Even though their language and music were forbidden, the Africans developed a musical style based on European traditions. This style allowed them to "talk" to one another, much as they had done in the lands that most would never see again. Some of the musical qualities that Africa contributed to this union of cultures can be seen below.

QUALITIES OF AFRICAN MUSIC

1. **Importance of complex rhythm patterns**
2. **Importance of percussion instruments**
3. **Use of *polyrhythms* (two or more rhythms performed at the same time)**
4. **Rhythm patterns repeated over and over**

MUSIC OF TWO WORLDS

Think of African music. What do you hear? You probably hear **rhythm**—lots of rhythm! Of course, you may say that all music has rhythm. Ah, but African rhythm is unlike that of any other music. What creates that unique excitement and drive that African music has?

Many African groups develop a **rhythm complex.** Following the chart below and using five nonpitched percussion instruments, you can perform a rough imitation of a rhythm complex. First recite the numbers in sequence to twelve over and over until you feel the **beat** securely. Then choose instruments and play only on the beat given in your rhythm line. For example, player A will play only on beats 1, 4, 7, and 10. Start slowly and eventually work up to a very fast rhythm. Try adding other instruments and making up new rhythm patterns.

RHYTHM COMPLEX

	1	2	3	4	5	6	7	8	9	10	11	12
A	1			4			7			10		
B		2	3		5	6		8	9		11	12
C	1		3		5	6		8		10	11	
D	1		3		5	6	7			10		
E	1		3			6		8	9			12

● An English Song

African-American music evolved from the African slaves' overlay of American and European harmonic and melodic styles on African rhythm and percussive practices. It may have sounded strong in the beginning! Learn to sing "Oh, Dear! What Can the Matter Be?" and then listen on page 12 to what can be done with it.

Oh, Dear! What Can the Matter Be?

English Folk Song

Oh, dear! What can the mat-ter be? Dear, dear, what can the mat-ter be?

Oh, dear! What can the mat-ter be? John-ny's so long at the

fair._____ He prom-ised to bring me a bas-ket of po-sies, A

gar-land of lil-ies, A gift of red ros-es, A

lit-tle straw hat to set off the blue rib-bons That

tie up my bon-ny brown hair._____ Oh, dear!

What can the mat-ter be? Dear, dear, what can the mat-ter be? Oh, dear!

What can the mat-ter be? John-ny's so long at the fair._____

A Blend of These Two Worlds

Here is "Oh, Dear! What Can the Matter Be?" combined
with the rhythm complex. The rhythm complex is normally an
accompaniment for singing or dancing, so there is usually a melody
sung over it. Of course, it is doubtful that any African group ever
sang "Oh, Dear" to a rhythm complex. But it does seem likely that
American- and European-style melodies were sung to rhythm
complexes in this hemisphere.

 Oh, Dear! What Can the Matter Be? (with rhythm complex)

A Song of the Yoruba

In Nigeria the Yoruba (YAWR uh buh) group worships a household
god called Elegua. When the Yoruba crossed the ocean to Cuba they
brought their beliefs with them, so it was natural for a song to be
written about Elegua. Although the language is Spanish and the
harmonies Western, it is rhythmically African. Learn to sing
"Elegua," on page 13.

Yoruba tribesmen

Elegua

Words and Music by Eduardo Davidson   English Words by Samuele Maquí

E - le - gua,
eh - leh - gwah

E - le - gua, san - to bo - ni - to;*
eh - leh - gwah sahn - toh boh - nee - toh

E - le - gua,
eh - leh - gwah

E - le - gua, san - to chi - qui - to.†
eh - leh - gwah sahn - toh chee - kee - toh

E - le - gua, ca -
eh - leh - gwah kah -
E - le - gua, you

ba - llo ne - gro____ con ban - de - ra co - lo - rao.
bah - yoh neh - groh kohn bahn - deh-rah koh - loh - rau
ride a black horse____ and car - ry a scar - let flag.

E - le - gua, ca -
eh - leh - gwah kah -
E - le - gua, you

ba - llo ne - gro____ con ban - de - ra co - lo - rao.
bah - yoh neh - groh kohn bahn - deh - rah koh - loh - rau
ride a black horse____ and car - ry a scar - let flag.

*lovely saint   †little holy doll

Your Own Rhythm Complex

You can make up your own rhythm complex. Here are the
beginnings of it. You might play it using a cowbell on line A and
maracas on line B.

```
    1 2 3 4 5 6 7 8
A.  1   3   5   7
B.  1 2 3 4 5 6 7 8
C.
D.
E.
```

Now, place numbers at random in the blank spaces. Don't use too
many! There need to be spaces between the sounds to make your
rhythm complex really interesting. Work out your rhythm complex
and use it to accompany *Gitano,* performed by the group Santana.

LISTENING LIBRARY

Gitano . . . . Peraza

A Blend of Two Worlds   **13**

THE INFLUENCE GROWS

In this recording you will hear two singers. One is an African-American folk singer from Mississippi. The other is a singer from Upper Volta, a country on the west coast of Africa. What do you hear that is different in these songs? What is alike? Listen to the way both singers ornament the melodies. They slide up and down on the **pitches,** sometimes not even singing the exact pitches at all!

 African-American and West African Vocal Styles

Now listen to Aretha Franklin singing *Soulville.*

Can you hear anything in her vocal style that is like that of the two folk singers?

 Soulville ... Turner, Levy, Glover, and Washington

Aretha Franklin

The Jazz Drummer

You've heard the word *polyrhythm* before. African music is filled with it. Your rhythm complex was a good example of polyrhythms in action. In the style known as "hot jazz"—jazz that is loud, fast, and rhythmic—the drummer may be the most important member of the **ensemble,** for it is this person who keeps those African-inspired polyrhythms going. Listen to this drummer as he unleashes his polyrhythms in a furious drum solo.

 Drum solo—jazz style

Phil Collins

Change the beat somewhere and the drummer can provide a rock rhythm background. Can you hear how the rhythms change in the rock-style solo?

 Drum solo—rock style

And how about our Latin American rhythms? They, too, are African in origin. In many ways they are more openly African than our American jazz or rock rhythms are. That is because, unlike slaves in the United States, slaves in Latin America were allowed to retain their cultural traditions. Latin American slaves had no need to alter their music as much as slaves in North America did.

 Drum solo—samba

WHENCE JAZZ?

The Modern Jazz Quartet

Cultural traditions are so deeply ingrained in all of us that we can't help carrying them with us wherever we go. Even within the United States, if we move from one part of the country to another, we may find some cultural differences and bewildering habits. Other people may find our habits bewildering as well.

Slowly, however, we begin to blend our cultural patterns with those of the surrounding cultures. The African slaves did the same thing. Their music—rhythmic, driving, exciting—mixed with the European-based harmonies of the New World. That resulted in new kinds of music, including the only purely American musical style, **jazz.**

CALL CHART 1

Listen to Benny Goodman's *Seven Come Eleven*. It certainly doesn't sound African, but the many layers of complex rhythms plus the musicians' **improvisations** are reflections of the African musical heritage. The Call Chart will help you identify each instrument.

Seven Come Eleven . . . . Goodman

1. Drum set
2. Bass
3. Saxophone and vibraphone play theme
4. Clarinet improvisation with vibraphone accompaniment
5. Saxophone and vibraphone play theme
6. Guitar improvisation with vibraphone
7. Guitar with resonating vibraphone accompaniment
8. Guitar with vibraphone
9. Vibraphone improvisation with light clarinet accompaniment
10. Vibraphone improvisation
11. Clarinet improvisation
12. Saxophone and vibraphone play theme, ending in coda

Benny Goodman

THE GAME IS CALLED BY THE RIFFEREE

Riff! A most important characteristic of jazz. A riff is an **ostinato** (ah stee NAH toh), a pattern that repeats over and over. *Seven Come Eleven* has several riffs. Here are some of the more noticeable ones. If you listen to the Call Chart on page 17 again, you will hear these riffs at the calls shown.

Call 2

Calls 3, 5, 12

Call 6

● Improvising, or "Making It Up"

In the recording on page 14, you heard how African and African-American musicians made up music with their voices. Making up music on the spot is called *improvising*. African musicians also improvise on percussion instruments. And, as you have learned, African vocal improvisation was picked up in this country by instrumental musicians. What a curious development—an African vocal style that became a North American instrumental style!

In jazz, everyone improvises, whether the musician plays a pitched or a nonpitched instrument. Jazz players improvise on a chord scheme. A **chord** is any three or more notes with different letter names sounded together. But in jazz the chords have to be very specific. You will need five chords to improvise on *Seven Come Eleven*. Line up bells so that they look like those on page 19.

In this chart each box represents a **measure**. One student will be
assigned to each chord. When your turn comes, improvise a rhythm
on the chord during that measure. You can play two or three notes
at once or just play up and down the bells.

Section

A	$A^\flat$	$A^\flat$	$A^\flat$	$A^\flat$	$A^\flat$	$A^\flat$	$A^\flat$	$A^\flat$
A	$A^\flat$	$A^\flat$	$A^\flat$	$A^\flat$	$A^\flat$	$A^\flat$	$A^\flat$	$A^\flat$
B	C^7	C^7	F^7	F^7	$B^{\flat 7}$	$B^{\flat 7}$	$E^{\flat 7}$	$E^{\flat 7}$
A	$A^\flat$	$A^\flat$	$A^\flat$	$A^\flat$	$A^\flat$	$A^\flat$	$A^\flat$	$A^\flat$

You can improvise with the musicians on *Seven Come Eleven,* using
this chord pattern. Here is *Seven Come Eleven* without call
numbers. Listen for the drum and bass introduction and begin
playing when the saxophone begins (call 3 in the Call Chart).

Seven Come Eleven (without call numbers)..... Goodman

SYNCOPATION

Listen to this recording of "Comedy Tonight." What do you notice
about the rhythm of the words and music?

A Funny Thing Happened on the Way to the Forum,
"Comedy Tonight" .... Sondheim

There is a striking rhythm pattern that is heard again and again. It
can be written like this:

The pattern is *syncopated*. That is, strong emphasis is given to something that
should be weak. Here's the same pattern, this time without **syncopation**.

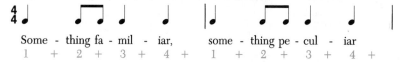

Compare the two versions. Syncopation gives an emphasis to the weak part of
the first beat of each measure and makes the music sound—well—jazzy! This
offbeat trick has been around for over 600 years, and African music certainly
focuses attention on it. Syncopation can change the character of a piece of music
entirely. On page 21 are two versions of the same song. Learn to sing it the way
it was originally written, then listen to the syncopated version. Can you
describe the differences?

A scene from "A Funny Thing Happened on the Way to the Forum"

You Are My Sunshine

Words and Music by Jimmie Davis and Charles Mitchell

Guitar: capo 3

You are my sun - shine, _____ my on - ly sun - shine;

_ You make me hap - py _____ when skies are gray. _____

_ You'll ne - ver know, dear, _____ how much I love you; _____

_ Please don't take my sun - shine a - way. _____

Syncopated version

1 + 2 + 3 + 4 + 1 + 2 + 3 + 4 +

You are my sun - shine, _ my on - ly sun - shine; _ You make me

hap - py _ when skies are gray. You'll nev - er know, dear, _

how much I love you; _ Please don't take my _ sun - shine a - way. _____

A PIECE THAT AFRICA INSPIRED

The percussion section! Our melodic instruments, such as the clarinet, flute, trumpet, and all the strings, are European in origin, but our percussion instruments owe much to Africa. The xylophone (with its relatives the vibraphone and marimba), the tom-tom, the maracas, the claves, the slit drum, the conga drum, and many others, are all derived from African influences. How much less interesting our American music might be today had it not been for the enrichment by Africans.

Afro-Amero, a piece for percussion ensemble, was inspired by Phil Faini's (fah EE nee) studies in Africa. It was composed so that school students could perform African rhythms, using instruments that might be found in the school percussion ensemble. There is a main melodic **theme** that looks like this. Play it on bells or on the piano.

Here is the main rhythmic theme written in the rhythm complex format. Try clapping or playing it on a nonpitched percussion instrument.

```
1  2  3  4  5  6  7  8  9  10  11  12
1     3     5  6     8     10  11
```

The Call Chart on page 23 will show you what happens in the piece.

West Virginia University Percussion Ensemble

CALL CHART 2

Afro-Amero .... Faini

1. Main rhythmic theme; marimba; main rhythmic theme again

2. Melodic theme appears; slow tempo

3. Loud main rhythmic theme; *p,* followed by layering of rhythms

4. Timpani

5. Tom-tom leading to (>) sudden stop; short, sharp patterns and silences

6. Rhythmic theme and melodic theme at the same time; melody, in smaller note values, moves faster now; again sudden stop; short, sharp patterns and silences

7. Strong rhythm ♩♪♪♪♩♪♪♩♪♪ ; timpani begin a layering of rhythms

8. Melody, in still smaller note values, moves even faster; energetic rhythm of call 7 reappears *ff*

9. Layering of rhythms (polyrhythms), ◁ *ff*

10. Melody in even smaller note values and slightly syncopated; ◁ coda

STYLE CONSCIOUS

"That's a new style."

"The costumes were in the style of the 1920s."

What, do you suppose, is meant by expressions such as these? *Style* is something that affects our lives in many ways, yet we are often unaware of how it influences us.

What *is* style? *Style* is the appearance of an object (a painting, a building, a suit of clothes) or even the look of a certain dance. Everything has style. There may be differences in style within the same time period (as seen in the automobile pictures, for example), but it is usually easier to distinguish differences in style when the objects are from different time periods (as in the two buildings).

Fallingwater (Bear Run, Pennsylvania)

Monticello (Charlottesville, Virginia)

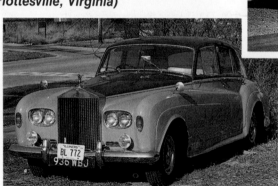

Music, too, has styles. They usually last longer than clothing or automobile styles. They last so long that we usually group them into large time periods and give them names. For example, the Classic period includes music that was written in Classic style. And the Modern period includes music in Modern style.

Here are two short excerpts from compositions that are rather long. Listen first to the overall "sound" of each piece.

 Concerto No. 21 in C Major for Piano and Orchestra, Movement 2 (excerpt) . . . . Mozart

 Concerto for Piano and Orchestra, Movement 1 (excerpt) . . . . Schoenberg

Each piece has an obvious **melody.** Follow the melodies as you listen to them again.

And each piece has some simple accompanying **harmony.**

Schoenberg, *Piano Concerto* © MCMXLIV by G. Schirmer, Inc. International Copyright Secured. Printed in the U.S.A.

The pieces sound very different in their melodies and harmonies, even though there are some similarities. Both **concertos** are written for a piano soloist with an orchestra of strings, winds, and percussion. What is different about these pieces is their *style.* One, by Mozart, is written in Classic style—a style that prevailed from about 1750 to about 1815. The other, by Schoenberg (SHUHRN behrg), is in a more **dissonant** twentieth-century style, a *modern* style.

MUSIC IN STYLISH CLOTHING

The clothing in the picture below is from the twentieth century. What is it about the clothes that makes you know they are from our time period? There is something about the materials, the cut, and the casual look of the clothing that tells you, "This is mine. This is from my time." Sometimes it's hard to describe exactly how we recognize a style from our time period. Perhaps books, magazines, movies, and television have made us familiar with the clothing of other eras so that we can compare them with our own clothing. For instance, the men in the pictures on page 27 are both wearing suits, but one suit is obviously from the twentieth century, and the other is from the Classic period.

It seems obvious that recognizing clothing styles is largely a matter of making comparisons. Recognizing musical styles is no different. We can compare and contrast two pieces of music, finding out the likenesses and the differences. Then we can make a judgment about these styles.

What exactly do we compare? We have to look at the specifics of our pieces—melody, harmony, rhythm, words (if the pieces are vocal works), tone color, and any other clue we might detect to help us see likenesses and differences.

MAKING COMPARISONS

Here is a song you can sing. Listen to the recording and follow the words and music. Then try singing along with the recording or with the piano accompaniment that your teacher or another student might play.

Where Have All the Flowers Gone?

Words and Music by Pete Seeger

Guitar: capo 5

1. Where have all ___ the flow - ers gone, ___ Long time ___ pass - ing, ___
2. Where have all ___ the young girls gone, ___ Long time ___ pass - ing, ___

Where have all ___ the flow - ers gone, ___ Long time a - go,
Where have all ___ the young girls gone, ___ Long time a - go,

Where have all ___ the flow - ers gone, ___ Young girls ___ picked them ev - 'ry one. ___
Where have all ___ the young girls gone, ___ Gone to young men ev - 'ry one, ___

When will they ev - er learn, _____ when will they ev - er learn?
When will they ev - er learn, _____ when will they ev - er learn?

3. Where have all the young men gone, long time passing. . .
   Where have all the young men gone, they are all in uniform. . .

4. Where have all the soldiers gone, long time passing. . .
   Where have all the soldiers gone, gone to graveyards ev'ry one. . .

5. Where have all the graveyards gone, long time passing. . .
   Where have all the graveyards gone, covered with flowers ev'ry one. . .

6. Where have all the flowers gone. . .

Now listen to the next piece. It is a piece by Haydn, a Classic-period composer. What comparisons can you make between this piece and "Where Have All the Flowers Gone?"

St. Anthony Chorale .... Haydn

You've sung the song and listened to *St. Anthony Chorale*. Let's look at a chart to see the likenesses and the differences in the two pieces.

	'Where Have All the Flowers Gone?	*St. Anthony Chorale*
Tone Color	Voice and Piano	Organ
Melody	Clear, strong melody	Clear, strong melody
Rhythm	Relaxed; sometimes on the beat, sometimes syncopated	On the beat, like a hymn or patriotic song
Harmony	Harmony is an accompaniment to the singer	Mostly three or four basic chords
Form	Simple phrase repetition with slight variations on phrase endings	ABA

Wes Montgomery, a guitarist, has put the two pieces together. The *Chorale* is always played by trumpets; the guitar plays "Where Have All the Flowers Gone?" Listen to the way Montgomery blends the eighteenth and twentieth centuries.

Where Have All the Flowers Gone? .... Seeger

SIMPLICITY THEN AND NOW

Westward ho! Manifest Destiny! Go West, young man! These are all phrases that led thousands and thousands of men and women in America to move westward in the nineteenth century. The people traveled on horseback and in covered wagons. Many simply *walked* across the prairies and mountains to find homes in the western territories of the young United States.

The Indians, native peoples who had dwelled on the continent for centuries, resisted with fury the encroachment on their land. This dramatic period in the history of the United States is reflected in countless **folk songs** and **ballads.** The music has a similarity of harmony, easy-to-sing melodies, and simple rhythms that fall mainly on the beat, like the three cowboy songs in the **medley,** "Songs of the West."

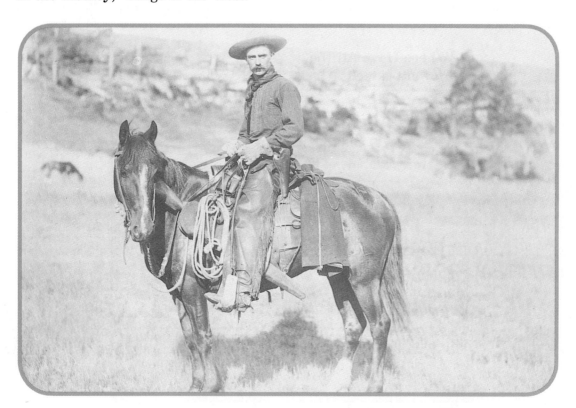

Songs of the West

Arranged by Linda Williams

Red River Valley

1. From this val-ley they say you are go-ing, _____ We will
   sit by my side if you love me, _____ Do not

2nd Time Only

   sit by my side if you love me, _____ Do not

miss your bright eyes and sweet smile;_____ For they say you are tak - ing the
has - ten to bid me a - dieu;_____ But re - mem-ber the Red Riv - er

has - ten to bid_ me a - dieu, a - dieu; But the Red Riv - er

sun - shine_____ that bright-ens our path - way a - while. 2. Come and
Val - ley_____ And the

Val - ley And the 2. Come and

girl. . . . 1. As I_walked out in the streets of La - re - do, As
you are a cow-boy," These

girl who has loved you so true. Slow - ly,

I walked out in La - re - do one day, I spied a young cow-boy wrapped
words he said as I bold - ly walked by. "Come lis - ten to me and I'll

play the fife low - ly. He was a young

fier - y and snuff - y are rar - in' to go.

fier - y and snuff - y are rar - in' to go. For the fier - y and snuf - fy are

SOLO

From this val - ley they say you are go - ing. *rit.*

rar - in' to go. From this val - ley you are go - ing. *ALL rit.*

CALL CHART 3

Here is a Call Chart on a piece from the Classic period. Listen to the composition as you follow it. How does this music compare to the songs in "Songs of the West"? Like the cowboy songs, it has a similarity of harmony, simple (that's the word!) melodies, and simple rhythms that fall mainly on the beat.

LISTENING LIBRARY

Sonata No. 15 in C Major, K. 545, Movement 1 (excerpt) .... Mozart

1 First theme outlines chords

2 Scale passages upward and downward
3 Second theme

4 Chord passages—chords outlined
5 Closing passage, getting ready for the end

How Different Is Different?

Make a chart to show the similarities and differences between "Chester" and "NonChester." You can copy the chart below on a separate sheet of paper.

	"Chester"	"NonChester"
Rhythm, Beat		
Meter		
Form		
Note Value		
Melody Steps		
Leaps		
Singing Voice		
Speaking Voice		
Unusual Vocal Sounds		

Chester

Words and Music by William Billings

1. Let ty - rants shake their i - ron rod,
2. What grate - ful off' - ring shall _____ we bring,

And slav - 'ry clank _____ her gall - ing chains;
What shall we ren - der to _____ the Lord?

We fear them not, We _____ trust _____ in God;
Loud hal - le - lu - jahs _____ let _____ us sing,

New _____ Eng - land's God _____ for - ev - er reigns.
And _____ praise His name _____ on ev - 'ry chord.

NonChester

Words by William Billings   Music by Mary E. Hoffman

EVEN SYMPHONIES HAVE THEIR DIFFERENCES

"Chester" and "NonChester" have one thing in common—the words.
Otherwise, one is hymnlike and solemn; the other is filled with
different vocal sounds and erratic rhythms. Listen to these next two
pieces. They, also, are in different styles. After you have listened to
them, decide which list below most closely describes the Mozart
piece and which list most closely describes the Shostakovich piece.

Symphony No. 40 in G Minor, Movement 3 . . . . Mozart

Symphony No. 1 in F, Movement 2 . . . . Shostakovich

	List 1	List 2
TONE COLOR	Full orchestra	Full orchestra, some piano
HARMONY	Little dissonance	Some dissonance
METER	Meter in 3	Meter in 2
MELODY	Singable	Not very singable
TEMPO	Tempo remains the same throughout	Tempo changes from fast to slow to fast

Mozart lived and composed during the Classic period—the latter
half of the eighteenth century and the early nineteenth century.
Shostakovich was a twentieth-century composer. He is a
contemporary composer. Both men used the same musical materials,
the same building blocks—pitch, rhythm, meter, tone color, and so
forth. But the different ways they put these building blocks together
created their different styles.

time TIME   color COLOR   meter METER

rhythm RHYTHM

pitch PITCH

Wolfgang Amadeus Mozart
(1756–1791)

Mozart began his musical studies at an early age with his father, Leopold. Under Leopold's guidance young Wolfgang and his older sister, Nannerl, toured Europe as performers. One story told of Wolfgang (although probably just a legend) says he appeared before the royal family in Vienna. So taken was he with the young princess Marie Antoinette (who, as Queen of France, would lose her head during the French Revolution) that he leaped into her lap vowing to marry her when he grew up! Only a story, perhaps, yet it suggests the impact the gifted child must have had.

Mozart wrote in all the forms of the Classic period, enriching the world for centuries to come and representing the Classic period at its finest. His early death and his burial in an unmarked pauper's grave have not dimmed his brilliance.

Meet the Composer

Dimitri Shostakovich
(1906–1975)

Many feel that Shostakovich, a Soviet composer, is perhaps the finest symphony composer of the mid-twentieth century. His fifteen symphonies show not only a great deal of depth, but a struggle to be fresh and original without overstepping the bounds laid down by the government for a Soviet composer. The Soviet government insists that composers write within the style of "socialist realism"—a style that demands folk or folk-like elements, little dissonance, straightforward rhythms, simple harmonies, a patriotic element, and so forth.

In the beginning of his career, Shostakovich had composed in the dissonant style of the West, but the powerful Union of Soviet Composers, which policed such things, forced him to conform to the dictates of socialist realism. That Shostakovich was able to write such original works as his *Fifth Symphony* or the "Baba Yar" *Symphony* within the constrictions of socialist realism is a tribute to his genius.

THE CLASSIC PERIOD

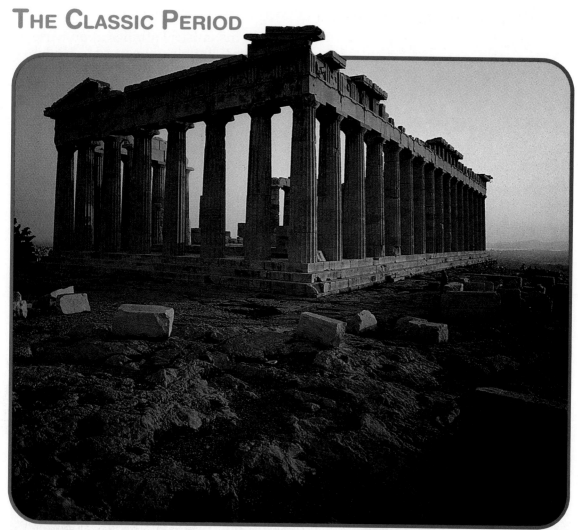

The Parthenon (Athens, Greece)

If you were asked to describe the building in this picture, what would you say about it? For one thing, it is beautifully proportioned. The columns are precisely placed to provide strength yet give a feeling of lightness, balance, and equality. The lines are clean and the decorations subtle. The building, a very ancient building found in Athens and called the Parthenon, is one of the world's greatest examples of Greek classic architecture.

About the middle of the eighteenth century, people became interested in the classicism of ancient Greek art and architecture. Greek philosophy was studied for its "modern" applications. Many people were curious to find answers to all sorts of questions in philosophy, art, religion, music, science, and technology. This time has been called the Age of Enlightenment, or the Age of Reason. The attempt to resurrect the ancient Greek culture resulted in the new **Classic period**.

● Painting in the Age of Reason

David's (dah VEED) *The Oath of the Horatii* is considered by many to be among the finest examples of Classic paintings. The viewer can see at once that the number *three* is of great importance to the artist. There are three women at the right of the painting, and three young men are taking an oath. The angle of the swords forms a triangle. The legs of the men form other triangles, and there are three archways in the background. The positions of the people in the painting create a sense of balance. While two of the women are leaning to the right—out of the frame—the third is leaning in to the left, her head on the shoulder of her kinswoman, her body and head angled in toward the men. This creates a focus toward the center of the painting. The two children—just by the contrast of being only two—point up the pervading number three. Proportion and balance are key elements in the Classic style.

THE OATH OF THE HORATII   *Jacques-Louis David*

David, *The Oath of the Horatii,* The Toledo Museum of Art, Toledo, OH

HOW DO YOU KNOW IF IT'S CLASSIC?

When you listen to a song on the radio, you can usually tell whether it's a rock song, a piece of jazz music, a Broadway show song, or a folk song. Sometimes you can even tell if the song was written in the 1920s or 1930s, the 1950s or 1970s, even the 1980s. That's because each type of song has its own style—those characteristics that set it apart in sound.

The music of the Classic period also has its own sound and style. Let's try putting a Classic piece together bit by bit. Here is a short melodic fragment. Sing it or play it.

Example 1

It doesn't sound finished, does it? It's too short. It needs something to balance it. Remember that Classic music is known for its sense of balance, of symmetry. So sing or play each of the following fragments. Which one seems to balance the first fragment best?

Example 2

Example 3

Example 4

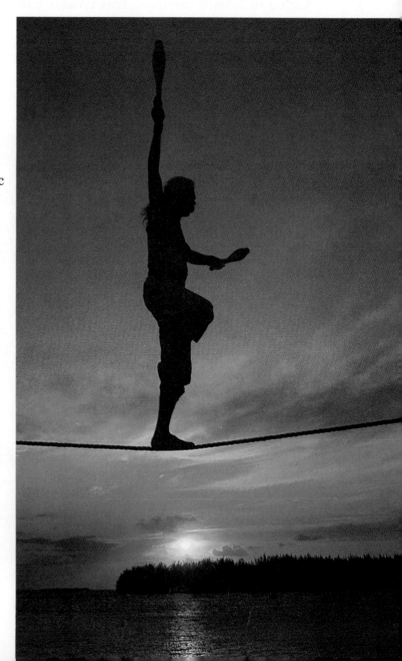

Examples 2 and 4 don't seem to work. The shape of the melody is all wrong, and the notes don't seem to wind up in the right place. Example 3, on the other hand, is a good balance to Example 1. The melodic shape is exactly the same as in Example 1 but placed one pitch lower. Now it looks like this.

Example 5

You, your teacher, or another student can play the example on the piano or on bells.

A rhythm pattern adds interest to the melody.

Example 6

● A New Phrase

Our rhythm pattern continues, even though a new **phrase** is introduced. The composer has balanced the second phrase in a different way. The melody goes up until the middle of the phrase; then it goes down, still using the rhythm pattern. The rhythm pattern becomes a unifier, an element that holds everything together.

Phrase 1

Phrase 2

● Adding Harmony

Our song is in the **key** of B♭. That means that notes in it are based on the B♭-major **scale.** On the **staff,** the B♭-major scale looks like this.

Line up your bells on the B♭ scale and play it up and down to hear its "sound." Now set up those groups of bells like this.

These chords are called **triads.** You can use them to add harmony to our Classic song. Try practicing the chords. Play this chord progression, using the B♭ and F triads.

Try singing along on the syllable *la,* using the first half of the phrase in Example 6 on page 41. Just as the melody seemed to need something to balance or complete it, the harmony seems unfinished as well. Try this progression on the second half of Example 6 on page 41. You will probably find it much more satisfying.

● All Together Now!

Now play the chords while your classmates sing.

To harmonize a second part of the song, you will want a new chord—the C-major triad. On the staff it looks like this.

Line up your bells to look like this.

You need the C-major chord because the composition changes to a new key, from B♭ to F. Changing key is one of the most characteristic elements of Classic style. You will hear it again and again in the Classic works of many composers.

We have been constructing a song by Wolfgang Amadeus Mozart. It is the **aria** "In the Army," from *The Marriage of Figaro*. Play the chords as your classmates sing. Watch the *D.S. al Fine*. That means to go back to the sign ℅ and sing to the word *Fine* (FEE nay).

The Marriage of Figaro is an **opera,** a play set to music. Opera audiences applaud after a soloist finishes an aria like "In the Army" as well as after major duets, choruses, or other ensembles.

In the Army

from *The Marriage of Figaro*

Music by Wolfgang Amadeus Mozart

Ludwig van Beethoven

1770—Beethoven is born.

1775—The American Revolution begins.

1776—The Declaration of Independence is ratified in Philadelphia.

1789—The French Revolution begins.

1791—The Bill of Rights becomes part of the Constitution of the United States of America.

1797—Franz Schubert is born.

1803—The Louisiana Purchase doubles the size of the United States.

1804—Nathaniel Hawthorne, America's first great novelist, is born.

1807—Beethoven's *Symphony No. 5 in C Minor* is completed.

1810—Beethoven's *Egmont Overture* is completed.

1812—The War of 1812, between the United States and Great Britain, begins.

1827—Beethoven dies in Vienna, Austria.

● Musicians Now and in Beethoven's Time

Musicians today have many outlets for their profession. Rock bands, church and synagogue choirs, orchestras, theaters, dance bands, and recording studios all provide opportunities for the working musician to earn a living. Some composers write for Broadway, for films and television, for opera houses, or for choruses and orchestras. Many musicians teach privately. Others teach in public or private schools, in colleges, conservatories, and universities. Your own music teacher is one of these teaching musicians.

Music editors

Music teacher

Opera singer

Rock musician (Bruce Springsteen)

Composer

● A Servant Class

In Beethoven's time, musicians were of the servant class. They usually served as church musicians or as "house" composers and conductors in the palace homes of the aristocracy. It was a secure job, usually meaning a small but steady income for life. Beethoven's father and grandfather had served the elector Franz Joseph, and everyone expected that young Ludwig, learning the viola and harpsichord with his father as his teacher, would follow his elders into the elector's service. From that beginning he would become the composer who, in many opinions, was one of the three or four greatest composers in history.

"A Chamber Concert at Sans Souci"

Beethoven's Youth

Beethoven performing before Prince Louis Ferdinand of Prussia

When we read about the growing-up years of famous composers, their childhoods so often seem to have been unhappy ones. Beethoven's early years were no exception. His alcoholic and overbearing father made a habit of waking the young Ludwig in the middle of the night, making him practice on the violin, viola, and at the pianoforte (as the early pianos were called) until sunrise. The exhausted boy was even discouraged from writing his own music. Instead the elder Beethoven insisted that his talented son practice only in preparation for his music lesson.

In spite of his father, young Beethoven managed to develop his considerable talent. He became an assistant organist and a violinist in the local court chapel and orchestra, positions that helped him to learn about the major composers of his time and about the instruments of the orchestra.

BEETHOVEN, THE WRITER OF SONGS

Beethoven was not famed as a writer of songs, but this small **round** is typical of his sound and style.

The Metronome

Music by Ludwig van Beethoven   English Words by Georg von Sudland

Tick, tock, tick, tock, tick, tock, tick, tick-a tock, tick-a tock, tick-a tock, The met-ro-nome is_count-ing. Tick, tock, tick, tock, tick, tock, tick, tick, tock, Hear it count the time. Tick, tock, tick, tock, tick, tock, tick, tick, tock, Count-ing the tem-po and the time that it takes to per-form. Tick, tock, tick, tock, tick, tock, The might-y met-ro-nome is march-ing, march-ing, march-ing on.

● **Beethoven the Idealist**

Beethoven's fame as a pianist spread quickly, and his reputation as a composer would soon grow to that of greatness. At the same time the ideals of the French Revolution of 1789—liberty, equality, and the fellowship of humankind—began to alter philosophical, social, and political thinking all over Europe. Beethoven, now a young man, found these principles of personal freedom deeply affecting. They would influence his choice of musical subjects until the end of his life, in such works as the *Symphony No. 9*, with its "Ode to Joy"; the opera *Fidelio;* and the *Egmont Overture*.

Beethoven and the Duke of Egmont

Beethoven's love of freedom drew him to a play by Goethe (GUHR tuh), the great German poet and playwright. The play's background is the revolt of the Dutch against their Spanish oppressors during the sixteenth century.

To support his growing empire, King Philip of Spain seized the Netherlands. The Dutch revolt in 1566 brought in the Spanish duke of Alba to crush the rebellion. The duke had thousands of people tortured and killed.

Now appeared the Duke of Egmont, a Dutch nobleman whose defiance of Alba led him to the gallows. In Goethe's play, Egmont's wife, Clarchen (CLAHR khehn), visits him in a dream as he lies in his cell waiting for execution.

"Your death will inspire the Dutch to rise up against the Spanish and overthrow them," she tells the awestruck Egmont. And at the gallows the next morning, he calls upon the Dutch to take pride in their heritage and win freedom for themselves once again.

CALL CHART 4

Listen to a Call Chart on the Overture to *Egmont*. The number will help you discover what is happening in the music.

Egmont Overture . . . . Beethoven

2. As at beginning   3.   4. Egmont's theme

6. New theme
7. Egmont's theme
8. Same as 5

11. Full orchestra

THE ROMANTIC PERIOD

"I'm an individual, and I'm going to do my own thing."

"I need to express myself in my own way and for myself alone."

"When I compose, I want to use more instruments and write for the largest orchestra ever!"

"The piano is my instrument of choice. I'll write piano music of technical brilliance!"

These are not the sentiments of young twentieth-century composers. These were the sentiments of composers who lived in the nineteenth century, a period we know as the **Romantic period.** The composers in the Romantic period were interested in expanding the whole musical vocabulary. Harmony became thick with notes, and dissonance began to play a more expressive part. Long melodies were written to provoke a strong emotional response. Form was expanded to become a loose framework on which to hang the beautiful melodies and harmonies. Listen to a piano piece by Liszt. Can you hear these characteristics in this work?

Concert Etude No. 3 in D♭ Major ("Un Sospiro") .... Liszt

Meet the Composer

Franz Liszt
(1811–1886)

Franz Liszt was the first solo concert performer. His piano virtuosity reshaped forever the way composers would think about this truly Romantic instrument. In the *Etude* "Un Sospiro" by Liszt you heard a broad melody sustained by an accompaniment of notes that seemed to cascade from the instrument. And you heard harmonies that were intended to make the listener feel deeply about the music. Liszt, along with Schubert, Schumann, and Chopin, was a typical example of the Romantic composer. He was a flamboyant figure who led a life that we associate today with movie stars or rock stars. Yet, he had a religious need (also typically Romantic) that led him to take minor orders in the Roman Catholic Church. To the end of his life he was called "Abbé Liszt" ("Father Liszt").

A Romantic Song

Johannes (yoh HAH n's) Brahms was a friend of Liszt and was a famous nineteenth-century composer himself. He wrote many pieces for all kinds of instrumental combinations. Many people like his songs best, especially his settings of folk songs. Romantic-period composers were fond of folk music and tried to incorporate it into their music.

Learn to sing "How Troubled the Waters." How is it different from the Classic pieces you have heard?

How Troubled the Waters

German Folk Song   Arranged by Johannes Brahms   English Version by Rosemary Jacques

1. How — trou-bled the wa - ters that run through the val - ley, And how
2. Though your words say your love will be true to me ev - er, Still I
3. I can tell you a thou - sand times how much I love you, But if

trou - bled am I, — I know we must part.
won - der, I won - der, the words have no heart.
you won't be - lieve me, then I can - not stay.

4. The friendship you gave me   And I pray that a true love
I'll always remember,   May soon come your way.

Meet the Composer

Johannes Brahms
(1833–1897)

Johannes Brahms wrote far more than songs. His four symphonies are considered among the best of the Romantic period. While still a young man, Brahms had the good fortune to be befriended by the German composer Robert Schumann, with whom he lived and studied. This friendship (along with that of Robert's wife, Clara, who was a fine composer and concert pianist herself) tied Brahms to one of the first great composers of the Romantic movement in music. He had the misfortune to be placed by the media, as well as by his supporters, in a musical rivalry with Richard Wagner. It was a rivalry neither Brahms nor Wagner felt, and each had only good words for the other.

THE TWENTIETH CENTURY—
OUR CONTEMPORARY PERIOD

At the time a piece of music is written, it is always "contemporary."
Contemporary is a big word meaning "with the times." We are living
in the latter part of the twentieth century. This is *our* contemporary
period. The twentieth century has seen many style changes in
printing, music, architecture, and clothing, just to name a few areas.
Look at the baseball uniforms above. The one on the left is from the
beginning of our century. The one on the right is from more recent
years. You see they are both baseball uniforms, because the basic
form is the same. But they are different in certain details. The caps
are different, as are the sleeves and trousers. Yet they are both
products of the twentieth century—our own century. How do you
think baseball uniforms will look a century from now?

If the twentieth century could be called anything at all (as the eighteenth century was called the Age of Reason), it might be called the Age of Technology. Everything in our society has been touched by the technological achievements of our century. The upper stamp below commemorates Wilbur and Orville Wright's first "flying machine" (the term *airplane* did not appear until several years later). This grand technological achievement of 1903 eventually led to the event commemorated in the bottom stamp below, the landing of a man on the moon on July 20, 1969.

Think of other technological developments of our century— the supersonic jet plane, new communication systems, the automobile, the X ray, television, computers, compact discs. Imagine someone from the eighteenth century suddenly waking up today! Sounds like an idea for a TV sitcom. Changes are happening so fast we can hardly keep track of them. Can you name any performing group that was on the Top 40 charts five years ago? Three years ago? Last year? Last month? Things are happening fast in music, too.

THE TWENTIETH-CENTURY VOICE

Ella Fitzgerald

Our century has been marked by countless experiments in finding new sounds. Sometimes the sounds have come from standard instruments. Jazz singers have developed a technique called *scat singing.* They use no words, only syllables, and the effect is like that of an instrumental solo. Listen to Ella Fitzgerald as she sings *Some of These Days* using scat syllables.

Some of These Days . . . . Brooks/Vogel

Sometimes composers have experimented with the human voice, asking it to do things not heard of until this century. Arnold Schoenberg, a composer in the first half of the twentieth century, asks the singer to create all sorts of new **vocal** effects in his song cycle *Pierrot lunaire* ("The Clown Pierrot by Moonlight"). Listen to "The Dandy" from this song cycle. In it Pierrot describes how he uses moonlight to paint his face so that he can look like a dandy— someone who is always well dressed, if a little overly so, and ready for a party. The vocal technique is called *Sprechstimme* (SHPREHKH shtih muh, or speech-voice), something that is part song, part speech.

Pierrot lunaire, "The Dandy" . . . . Schoenberg

A Graphic Score

The twentieth-century composition below calls for four kinds of vocal sounds: groans, hisses, lip pops, and sighs. Also, there is one pitch to be played on the piano (or any other instrument): C♯. The class can split into four sections to work out the piece. There is no meter, so watch the clock to time the sections. If a box is empty, do nothing. The thicker the line or the larger the symbol, the louder the sound. If a line is wavy, make the sound with a wide **vibrato** (vee BRAH toh). If a line or dot is high in the box, make a high sound. If it is low in the box, make a low sound. This kind of notation is called *graphic notation*. Have fun with it!

	5 Sec.	10 Sec.	5 Sec.	5 Sec.	10 Sec.	1 Sec.
Groan	—		▬ ▬ ▬		∿∿∿	▬
Hiss	– – – –	———	▬▬▬		– – – – – ·	▬
Lip Pop		• ● • • • ● •		• • • • · ·		●
Sigh		∿∿∿∿	∿∿∿		∿	▬
Piano		𝄞 ♯♪♪♪♪♪♪♪	𝄞 ♯♩ ♩		𝄞 ♯♪♪♪♪♪♪♪♪♪	𝄞 ♯♪

You can create your own piece using graphic notation. With your classmates, make up a vocal or instrumental sound for each symbol at the right. Put the symbols on the board in a specific order, then perform the piece. Try creating a piece for three or four independent voices or instruments.

MODERN DAYS, MODERN INSTRUMENTS (AND A FEW NEW TRICKS)

Did you ever think a radio could be a musical instrument?
Well, John Cage did. This highly original American
composer wrote a piece for twelve radios called
Imaginary Landscape, No. 4. Players tune to
any station and turn the volume up or down
as the conductor dictates. And how about
the tape recorder? Almost from the
beginning of tape-recording techniques,
composers have experimented with
creating new sounds using the
tape recorder. Listen to this
recording of a tape "classic"
by Canadian composer
Hugh LeCaine.
LeCaine used
a single drop
of water to create
all the effects.

Dripsody ....LeCaine

How could so many different sounds be created by a tape recorder?
Some ways were to record at one speed and play back at another,
making the sound higher or lower, and to edit the tape so that the
sounds were faster or slower, shorter or longer. Sometimes, LeCaine
put two versions of the drop together at the same time. You can be
sure that he spent many long hours at the tape recorder to create
this short, but to many people, fascinating piece.

Here are some experiments you can try with classroom instruments. You may find some sounds that are very unusual.

AUTOHARP

American composer David Eddleman created an autoharp piece by caressing the strings with a chamois (SHA mee) cloth, brushing the strings with a comb, plucking individual strings between the fingernails, and drawing an eraser across the strings, often while strumming. An unusual effect is created by holding down two chord bars, one a minor chord and the other a corresponding major chord (G major and G minor, for example). The result is an open fifth—like a triad, but with the third left out. Listen to *Autoharp Fantasy*.

 Autoharp Fantasy . . . . Eddleman

MALLET INSTRUMENTS

Put the mallets in each hand and play tone clusters (notes that are right next to one another, like C, D, and E) on xylophone, glockenspiel, or metallophone. Vary your mallets. Use a tennis ball or the eraser end of a pencil.

RESONATOR BELLS

With the bells in their case, lean close to them and sing any pitches. You will hear the bells responding. Sing your name into the bells, with long pauses between syllables—*Jess-* (pause) *-i-* (pause) *-ca* (pause)—and listen as the bells respond to your speaking voice. This effect will work even better using a piano with the damper pedal depressed.

PIANO

Take a ruler or your forearm and depress a whole cluster of keys. (Alternate between black key clusters and white key clusters.) Our friend John Cage startled the musical world some years ago by writing a piece for "prepared piano." The piano was prepared by placing various articles on the felts, or against the strings to alter the sound. Listen to *Dance,* for prepared piano. Do you think it still sounds like a piano?

 Dance. . . . . Cage

MELODY

So far, you would think all twentieth-century composers went out of their way to create new sounds. Not so. In 1917, Prokofiev wrote a **symphony** in the style of Mozart and Haydn (Remember them?). He called it *Classical Symphony* because he wanted to suggest the form and character of the late eighteenth-century symphony. Of course, it isn't exactly in the same style, because Prokofiev used melodic and harmonic styles that could only be from the twentieth century, with their sharp melodic turns and harmonic dissonances. Listen to the "Gavotte" from the *Classical Symphony,* and follow the line score.

Classical Symphony, Movement 3, "Gavotte"...Prokofiev

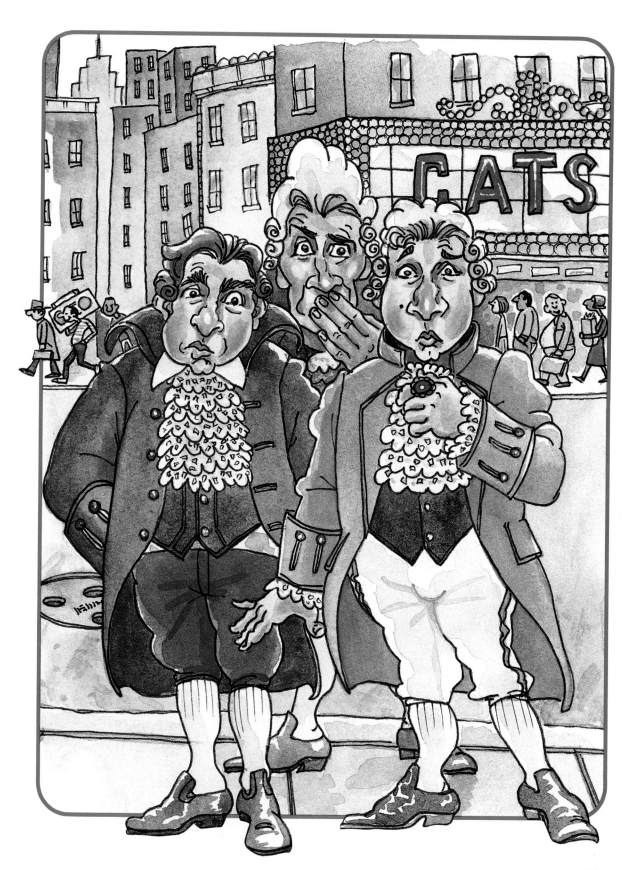

Melody, Melody, Who Has the Melody?

The melody in the "Gavotte" *might* be considered singable, but you would have a hard time singing it. The extreme range from top note to bottom, as well as the fragment with leaps, would make it a difficult singing piece.

Melodies of the twentieth century are hard to pin down. Some of them are singable in the old nineteenth-century way. Others are so untraditionally melodic that they are difficult to follow. In these pieces that feature the flute, what kinds of melodies do you hear?

Listening for Melodic Styles
Interpolations for Flute (excerpt) . . Haubenstock-Ramati

Irlandaise (excerpt) . . . . Bolling

Opus Vetrinus (excerpt) . . . . Eddleman/Roberts

Sonata for Flute, Movement 2 (excerpt) . . . . . . Hindemith

Or (excerpt) . . . . Dick

The flutist in the picture could be playing any one of these pieces, but what do the graphics on page 63 suggest about each melody?

Interpolations for Flute

Irlandaise

Opus Vetrinus

Sonata for Flute

Or

RHYTHMS TODAY

It may be that the rhythm practices of the twentieth century will be
known as the most revolutionary of its innovations. Through the
centuries, a slow and gradual development of melody and harmony
took place, but not even the new harmonic language of the twentieth
century could equal the burst of activity in rhythm. Listen to part of
the **finale** of Stravinsky's 1913 **ballet** *The Rite of Spring* to hear the
way the composer constantly keeps the listener off balance through
the use of shifting meters and *polyrhythms* (several rhythms played
at the same time).

The Rite of Spring, "Finale" (excerpt)........Stravinsky

Many composers followed Stravinsky's lead. They wrote in ever more complicated rhythmic styles. It finally took the computer to be able to realize some of these composers' complex rhythmic ideas.

The simple percussion piece notated below shows some of the ways a composer might vary an uncomplicated rhythm:

This rhythm is subjected to certain changes. Yet the resulting new rhythms still retain the basic character of the original rhythm.

Here is how to play the percussion piece:

• Choose a percussion instrument to play all the measures in a meter of 4.

• Choose a different percussion instrument to play all the measures in a meter of 3.

• Choose a third instrument to play all the measures in a meter of 2.

• In Section II, percussion players play the bottom part and everyone else chants the rhythms on *cha*.

• Everyone performs in the last measure.

HARMONY—WILD AND WACKY

Listen to these two short pieces for piano. One is by Beethoven, a Classic composer. The other is by Béla Bartók, a twentieth-century composer. As you listen, ask yourself how the harmonies differ.

Minuet in G .... Beethoven

Mikrokosmos, "Wrestling" .... Bartók

Could you hear that the harmony in the Beethoven piece was different than the harmony in the Bartók piece? When you listened to *The Rite of Spring* in the previous lesson, you heard some fairly unusual harmonies there as well. In the twentieth century, harmony, like every other element of music, evolved into something very different from what it had been in the preceding centuries. Some people are repelled by the new harmonies; others find them exciting and stimulating. Whatever your own feeling, harmony will never be the same after the experiments of the twentieth century.

In the 1940s, Elliott Carter, a twentieth-century American composer, wrote a piece on a *single* chord for flute, oboe, clarinet, and bassoon. Listen to what Carter did with the chord.

Etudes for Woodwind Quartet, No. 3 .... Carter

● **Tone Clusters**

Elliott Carter used one D-major chord as material for an entire composition. Other composers use chords of many notes. Some even use chords that have every note. Do you remember the piano **tone clusters** mentioned on page 59?

Try this. Take a ruler and depress as many piano keys as you can. Use the lower pitches of the piano. Charles Ives used this technique in his composition *Majority*. Notice how the clusters in the boxes are notated.

The Mass - es! _____ The Mass - es!

The Polish composer Krzysztof Penderecki (KREESH tohf pehn deh REHT skee) used string clusters in his piece *Threnody for the Victims of Hiroshima.* Listen to the piece and examine the last page from the **score.** You can see the big blocks that stand for the tone clusters in this all-strings work.

Threnody for the Victims of Hiroshima .....
..... Penderecki

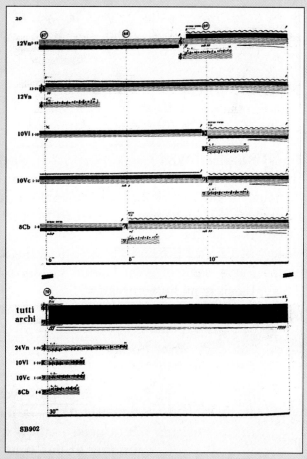

The Twentieth Century 67

TWENTIETH-CENTURY TONE COLOR

The synthesizer! Who hasn't heard it? It bleeps forth from almost every rock group and has now become an indispensable instrument. Curiously enough, this instrument—able to recreate the sound of any traditional instrument as well as to create brand-new sounds— found favor at first with "serious" composers. They manipulated the basic **wave forms** produced by the machine and created musical compositions, some of great length. Listen to some of the wave forms the synthesizer manufactures.

Wave Forms

- (a) Sine wave (low)—very pure sound
- (b) Sine wave (high)—very pure sound
- (c) Sawtooth wave—a nasal sound
- (d) White noise—not a wave form, but all frequencies sounding at one time. It sounds like a hiss.

CALL CHART 5

Listen to a piece that uses these wave forms. You will hear how
Raaijmakers (RYE mah kehrs) alters them to create organization and
interest. Follow the Call Chart to help you listen more clearly.

Contrasts (Part 2) . . . . Raaijmakers

1	INTRODUCTION	Filtered white noise in syncopated rhythm
2	SECTION A	Filtered white noise sweeping and popping in random sequence and bouncing back and forth from speaker to speaker, a low-pitched sine wave accompanies; later joined by higher pitched sine wave using a little "slide."
3	SECTION B	Increased activity of white noise pops and sweeps accompanied by a sawtooth wave ↗ ↘; syncopated white noise from introduction returns
4	SECTION A	Similar to call 2
5	CODA	Low-pitched sine wave with sawtooth wave ↗ ↘

Sound crazy? Not really. Raaijmakers has given us a piece that is
thoroughly worked out. It has been said that "the sky's the limit,"
and this is surely true of twentieth-century music. Listen to this
piece from a **suite** by Gustav Holst. He wrote it in 1916 (think of
Stravinsky and what *he* was doing about that time). The suite is
called *The Planets* and is a musical description of all the planets in
the solar system except Earth and as-yet-undiscovered Pluto. Our
selection is "Mercury," the "winged messenger." Isn't it amazing that
the Stravinsky piece, the Raaijmakers piece, and the Holst piece are
all products of our own century?

The Planets, "Mercury" . . . . Holst

GETTING A GOOD BLEND

Men and women have probably sung together in groups since people first developed music. That kind of group singing was probably only in **unison,** with all voices singing the same thing at the same time.

Our "modern" tradition of choral singing in many parts came out of the medieval church, in which men (and sometimes boys with unchanged voices) sang the service chants in unison. These chants—known as **plainsongs,** plainchants, or Gregorian chants (for Pope Gregory the Great, who lived from about 540 to 604)—had only one purpose: to point up the meaning of the religious text. Their "otherworldly" quality truly captured the mystery and sense of religious awe as practiced by the medieval church.

Listen to this plainsong selection. Can you hear how the voices blend, almost as if the men were singing with one voice? Look at the **notation** on page 71 from the Middle Ages. It looks very different from our modern-day notation. The little square notes are called *neumes.* Can you follow the neumes as you listen? (You can sing "Gaudeamus." The song is printed in modern notation on page 259.)

Gaudeamus omnes in Domino (excerpt)........Plainsong

"Old Hundred"

"Old Hundred" has been sung in the United States since the Puritans brought it over in 1628 in a book called *Whole Book of Psalms*.

Just as the monks blended their voices in the plainsong selection, try blending your voices as you sing "Old Hundred." Listen to your neighbor and try to match your voice to his or hers. Or as one teacher often puts it, "try to sing with the voice of the person next to you."

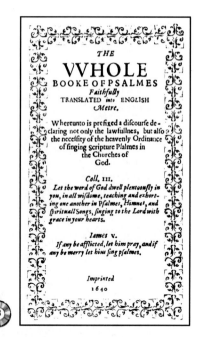

Old Hundred

Words by William Kethe   Music by Louis Bourgeois

1. All people that on earth do dwell,
Sing to the Lord with cheer - ful voice;
Him serve with fear, His praise forth tell;
Come ye be - fore Him and re - joice.

2. Oh, en - ter then His gates with praise,
Ap - proach with joy His courts un - to;
Praise, laud, and bless His name al - ways,
For it is seem - ly so to do.

You should have performed this song *a cappella* (without accompaniment). Did you stay on pitch, or did your pitch rise (go sharp) or fall (go flat)? It is necessary to listen carefully to be sure to stay on pitch.

MONOPHONIC AND POLYPHONIC TEXTURES

Do you see a connection between the melody of "Old Hundred" and this diagram?

If you recognized the outline of "Old Hundred," you were right. And since there is only one line of music, we call it *monophony* or **monophonic texture.** Monophony sounds like a ten-dollar word until you break it down—mono (one) phonic (from the Greek word *phones,* pronounced FOH nays, meaning "voice"), or one voice. The Gregorian chant, as well as "Old Hundred," is an example of monophonic texture.

As time progressed, musicians began to add other voices to the single-line plainchants. Usually, in the eleventh or twelfth centuries, the extra voices just sang the melody at a higher or lower interval. "Old Hundred," if it had been written then, would have looked like this in our graph.

This kind of texture took a new name. We call it **polyphonic**—from poly (many) phonic (again, from the Greek *phones*—"voice")—or many-voiced music. Listen to the way this kind of music sounds.

Rex caeli, Domine . . . . Ninth century polyphony

Creative composers found this note-against-note writing to be limiting. Eventually a new style of polyphonic choral writing developed. In this new style, each voice was independent and had a different melody from the other voices. Yet each voice contributed to the whole piece. The voices were independent, yet they were written so that they had no complete meaning without the other voices. Listen to the example of polyphonic music on the following pages and see if you can follow the vocal lines as they progress through the piece.

Kyrie

Words Traditional   Music by Antonio Lotti

le - i - son, _____ e - le - i - son.

son, e - le - - - i - son.

le - i - son, e - le - i - son.

le - - - - i - son.

Chri - ste e - le - i - son, e - le -

Chri - ste e - le - i - son, e - le -

DEVELOPING BREATH CONTROL

Most rounds that you sing are in polyphonic texture. The round below has many long phrases. You have to have good breath control to sing them! Your teacher will explain some good ways to get from one end of these lengthy phrases to the other end. You will occasionally see a comma (') above the music. The comma shows you where to take a breath. In the entire round there are only *two* breath marks.

The Hunter

Traditional

Guitar: capo 3

HOMOPHONIC TEXTURE

This chorale shows a different kind of texture. Here all the voices sing basically the same rhythm, with different notes for each voice. This kind of harmony is called *homophony* (hah MAH foh nee, meaning "same voice"), or **homophonic texture.** Even when one or two voices sing smaller notes, the other voices go on with the same rhythm. This hymn-like setting is placed on a **grand staff**—two staffs joined by a brace or bracket with treble clef for the top staff and bass clef for the bottom.

The King of Love My Shepherd Is

Psalm 23, from the *Scottish Psalter*   Irish Folk Melody   Harmonized by Daffyd Dylan

1. The king of love my shep-herd is, Whose good-ness fail-eth nev - er; I noth-ing lack if I am his And he is mine for-ev - er.

2. Where streams of liv - ing wa - ter flow, My ran-somed soul he lead - eth, And where the ver - dant pas - tures grow with food ce - les - tial feed - eth.

3. And so through all the length of days Thy good-ness fail - eth nev - er; Good shep - herd, may I sing thy praise with - in thy house for - ev - er.

SINGING PARTNER SONGS

Sometimes a song can be sung at the same time as another song. These partner songs can be fun to sing and will produce a type of polyphony that sounds different from some polyphonic music that you have heard or sung. Start off by learning to sing this song.

We're All Together Again

Traditional

We're all to-geth-er a-gain, we're here, we're here!__ We're all to-geth-er a-gain, we're here, we're here! Who knows when we'll be all to-geth-er a-gain, Sing-ing all to-geth-er a-gain, we're here, we're here!

(Whistle)

(Whistle)

Used by permission of the Boy Scouts of America.

When you have learned "We're All Together Again," learn to sing "While Strolling Through the Park" on the next page. You and your classmates can then sing the songs together as partner songs.

SUNDAY AFTERNOON ON THE ISLAND OF LA GRANDE JATTE

Georges Seurat

While Strolling Through the Park

Words and Music by Ed Haley

Guitar: capo 3

While ___ stroll - ing through the park one day, _____ In the
I im - med - i - ate - ly raised my hat, _____ And ___

mer - ry, mer - ry month of May, _____ I was tak - en by sur -
fi - nal - ly ___ she re - marked. ___ "I ___ nev - er shall for -

prise by a pair of ro - guish eyes, In a mo - ment my poor heart was stole a -
get that ___ love - ly af - ter - noon." I ___ met her at the foun - tain in the

way. _____ A smile ___ was all ___ she gave to me,
park. _____

of course we were as hap - py ___ as can be.

The Oratorio

Have you ever heard *Messiah,* by George Frideric Handel? The "Hallelujah" chorus is one of its best-known sections.

Messiah is an **oratorio**—a musical drama a little like an opera, but usually without costumes, scenery, or stage action. Unlike in opera, audiences usually do not applaud after each aria or chorus in an oratorio. They listen quietly and may applaud at the end. Handel, as well as many other composers, wrote a great number of oratorios. His oratorio *Judas Maccabaeus* is the story of the Maccabean struggle to rid Palestine of its Syrian oppressors. Listen to a chorus from *Judas Maccabaeus.* It uses all the textures that you have studied—monophonic, homophonic, and polyphonic. Can you recognize them?

Judas Maccabaeus, "Hallelujah, Amen" . . . . Handel

JUDAS MACCABAEUS   *Taddeo di Bartolo*

Taddeo di Bartolo: *Judas Maccabaeus,* 15th Century. Palazza Pubblico, Siena, Italy. Scala/Art Resource, NY.

SINGING AS A GROUP

You have practiced several singing techniques. Now, with your classmates, perform this song in unison as a choral group. Be aware of vocal blend ("singing with the voice of the person next to you"), watch **diction** and pitch, and try to exercise good breath control.

Dedication

English Version by Georg von Sudland   Music by Robert Franz

O, thank me not for songs I sing here, No gift of mine, they are your own. Yours was the gift, And I re-turn it, re-turn these songs to you a-lone. These songs were al-ways your pos-ses-sion, They sprang fresh from out your shin-ing eyes; There's where I heard them, there's where I learned them. Did you not know that each song is your own? Did you not know that each song is your own?

SINGING IN PARTS

Singing successfully in parts is a sign of musical independence. If you can "hold" your vocal part against someone else's different vocal part, it means you have developed a good ear and a good sense of harmony. Learn this part song. You might want to sing it in a concert sometime!

Water Come a Me Eye

Folk Song from Jamaica

1. Ev - 'ry time I 'mem - ber Li - za, Wa - ter come a me eye,
2. Since you gone the days are lone - ly, Wa - ter come a me eye,
3. When you here the time goes fast, —

When I think 'bout my gal Li - za,
Come back, gal, I love you on - ly, Wa - ter come a me eye.
Now you gone and love is past, —

REFRAIN

Come back, Li - za, come back, gal, — Wa - ter come a me eye.

Come back, Li - za, come back, gal, — Wa - ter come a me eye.

Printed by permission of Oxford University Press.

A German Folk Song

The German composer Johannes Brahms loved to make
arrangements of German folk songs. This one can be sung
as a choral song in two parts. Work out each part
separately, then put them together.

The Fiddler

English Version by Ruth Martin   Music by Johannes Brahms

1. A red-beard-ed fid-dler who lived on the Rhine
2. "You red-beard-ed fid-dler, now play us a tune,
3. The fid-dler struck up with his bow on the string,

Was walk-ing one night round a quar-ter to nine,
And we shall re-ward you both rich-ly and soon.
The la-dies danced round and round in a ring,

And on his way home, just guess what he saw, Just guess what he saw,
Bet-ter play us a dance that's mer-ry and light, That's mer-ry and light,
Then they all cri out with one ac-cord, With one ac-cord,

Not one pret-ty la-dy, but twen-ty or more!
For we have to cel-e-brate Wal-pur-gis Night."
"You've fid-dled so well you shall have your re-ward."

4. And while all the ladies applauded and cheered,
One brought out a scissors and cut off his beard.
"We've paid for your tune far more than it's worth,
    far more than it's worth,
We've made you the handsomest fiddler on earth!"

WHAT DO YOU HEAR? 1

Afro-Amero .... Faini

Listen to the recording and as each number is called circle the
correct answer.

1. Strong rhythm only   No rhythm alternates with
   strong rhythm

2. Fast tempo   Slow tempo

3. Loud, then soft   Soft only

4. Timpani   Flute

5. Tom-toms lead to short patterns   Long flowing melody

6. Melody is slower   Melody gets faster

7. Complete silence   Strong, irregular rhythm
   pattern

8. Melody much slower   Melody even faster

9. Polyrhythms   Only one rhythm on one
   instrument

10. Melody faster yet   Melody very slow and soft

TEST 1

Write the letter of the correct answer in the blank.

1. One of the qualities of African music is the use of _____.
   a. violins
   b. harpsichords
   c. complex rhythm patterns
   d. electronic effects

2. A rhythm complex consists of _____.
   a. several melodies sung together
   b. several rhythms played together
   c. a complicated rhythm pattern
   d. fear of rhythm

3. Two or more rhythms played at the same time are called _____.
   a. polyrhythms
   b. percussion
   c. countermelodies
   d. snare drums

4. The Yoruba group worshiped a household god called _____.
   a. Zeus
   b. Neptune
   c. Baal
   d. Elegua

5. African singers, as well as African-American folk singers, tend to _____ the melody.
   a. play
   b. write down
   c. ornament
   d. forget

Circle T if the statement is true; circle F if the statement is false.

6. Latin-American rhythms are less African than those in North America.

T   F

✓ TEST 2

Circle T if the statement is true; circle F if the statement is false.

1. Jazz is a blend of African rhythms and Western harmonies.

$$T \qquad F$$

2. Improvisation is a European, not an African style.

$$T \qquad F$$

3. A riff is a jazz name for an ostinato.

$$T \qquad F$$

4. In jazz, players improvise over a predetermined chord scheme.

$$T \qquad F$$

Write the letter of the correct answer in the blank.

5. Rhythmically, when strong emphasis is placed on something we expect to be weak, it is called _____ .

   a. beat   b. a quarter note
   c. meter   d. syncopation

6. Xylophones, marimbas, tom-toms, maracas, claves, slit drums, and conga drums are all _____ .

   a. string instruments   b. percussion instruments
   c. brass instruments   d. woodwind instruments

TEST 3

Circle the letter next to the correct answer.

1. What is *style*?
   a. a large hat   b. a beautiful house
   c. the appearance of an   d. a haircut
      object; the way it looks

2. A period of musical history usually has music written in basically the same style. One period is given below. Which is it?
   a. Baroque   b. Jazz
   c. Songs   d. Rock and Roll

3. Mozart was a Classic composer; Schoenberg composed during what period?
   a. the Classic period   b. the twentieth century
   c. the Renaissance period   d. the Baroque period

4. The music of the Classic period is clean, clear, and harmonious. How, generally, might you describe the style of the twentieth century?
   a. melodic   b. harmonically traditional
   c. dissonant   d. rhythmically square

Write the letter of the correct answer in the blank.

5. The Classic period has been called the Age of Enlightenment and the _____ .
   a. Age of Rocks   b. Age of Reason
   c. Age of Aquarius   d. Age of Gold

6. In Classic art, as well as in music, there is a great deal of attention to _____ .
   a. three   b. colors
   c. singing   d. proportion and balance

7. In the song "In the Army," two like sections are separated by an unlike section. This is called _____ .
   a. rondo form   b. a symphony
   c. ABA   d. a piano

8. Beethoven was greatly influenced by _____ .
   a. the American Revolution   b. the Thirty Years War
   c. the Mexican Revolution   d. the French Revolution

TEST 4

Circle T if the statement is true; circle F if the statement is false.

1. The Romantic period gave more importance to individual expression.

T   F

2. Franz Liszt was the first performer to give solo concerts.

T   F

3. Johannes Brahms was a good friend of Mozart.

T   F

4. *Sprechstimme* is a vocal technique that is part speech, part song.

T   F

Write the letter of the correct answer in the blank.

5. A type of notation that "draws pictures" of the kind of sound a performer should make is called _____ .
   a. style notation   b. classic notation
   c. graphic notation   d. scribbles

6. In *The Rite of Spring* Stravinsky wrote many rhythms to be played at the same time. This is called _____ . (Hint: You had this one in your study of African music.)
   a. synthesizer   b. polyrhythm
   c. tape recorder   d. multimeter

7. In *Threnody for the Victims of Hiroshima,* Penderecki uses lots of notes close together called _____ .
   a. polyrhythm   b. melodies
   c. saxophones   d. tone clusters

8. A synthesizer creates sound by manipulating _____ .
   a. wave forms   b. wave lengths
   c. wave bands   d. wave fronts

TEST 5

Circle the correct answer.

1. An ancient religious vocal form, sung in unison and notated in neumes.

   plainsong   art song   opera

2. What this kind of unison singing is called.

   monophonic   polyphonic

3. Adding a second voice at a different interval.

   polyphonic   voices

4. Many rounds are good examples of it.

   monophony   polyphony   atonality

5. Two or more voices singing the same rhythms, as in a hymn.

   monophony   polyphony   homophony

6. Two or more songs that can be sung together.

   art songs   partner songs   cowboy songs

7. A musical drama, usually with a great deal of choral work, but with no costumes, scenery, or stage action.

   opera   musical comedy   oratorio

8. In singing, careful attention to the clear pronunciation of the text.

   dynamics   interpretation   diction

UNDERSTANDING MUSIC

MELODY

When you think of music, what do you think of first? If you are like most people, you probably think first of *melody*. Have you ever found yourself leaving a concert or a musical play whistling or humming the tunes you just heard? Have you ever thought about a television show or a movie just because you recognized its theme song? When you did those things, you were responding to the melody, the element that usually most identifies a piece of music.

Harlech Castle (Wales)

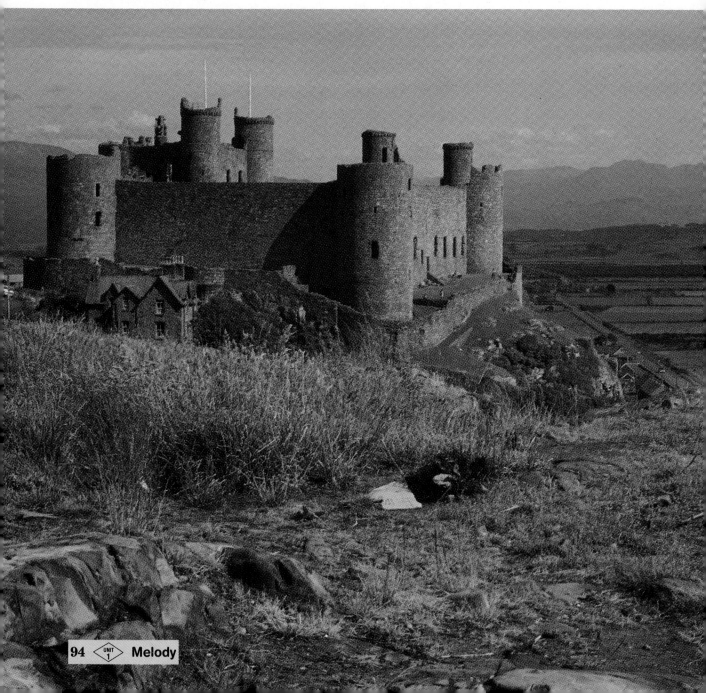

During the fifteenth century a famous castle in Wales—Harlech Castle, seen on page 94—came under siege. This song commemorates that battle. As you sing "Men of Harlech," pay attention to the way the melody flows upward and downward.

Men of Harlech

English Version by William Duthie   Traditional Welsh Song

Men of Har - lech, in the hol - low, Do ye hear, like rush - ing bil - low,

Wave on wave that, surg - ing, fol - low Bat - tle's dis - tant sound?

Loose the folds a - sun - der, Flag we con - quer un - der!

The plac - id sky now bright on high

Shall launch __ its __ bolts __ in __ thun - der!

On - ward! 'Tis our coun - try needs us; He is __ brav - est, he who leads us;

Hon - or's self now proud - ly heads us! Free-dom, God, and Right!

MELODY "STEPS" OUT

Melodies can move in three different ways.
They move by step when they are moving
along the *scale*. What is a scale? Look at this
example of a scale starting on the note C.

Each one of these notes is a step away from the note on either side.
They move from a line to the next space to the next line to the next
space, and so forth. As long as the notes move from a line to a
neighboring space or from a space to a neighboring line, the melody
is moving by step.

Listen to these examples of melodies moving by step.

Melodies Moving by Step

Prince Igor, "Polovtsian Dances" . . . . Borodin

The Nutcracker, "Grand Pas de Deux" . . . . . Tchaikovsky

On page 97 you will find a song that moves mostly by step. The
basic idea repeats over and over. When the song leaves the step
pattern, it can create a real surprise to the ears.

One of Those Songs

Guitar: capo 5

English Words by Will Holt   Music by Gerard Calvi

MELODY "LEAPS" ABOUT

Look at this scale passage. All the notes are moving by step. Play the passage on bells or on the piano.

C B A G F E D C

Now let's remove the notes shown in gray. Play the example on bells or piano leaving out the gray notes.

C A G E C

Do you hear the *leaps* in this passage?
When notes move from one line to any other line
or from one space to any other space, we call this "movement
by *leap*." Listen to these examples of melodies moving mostly by leap.

Melodies Moving by Leap

Skip to My Lou

Lou, Lou, skip to my Lou, Lou, Lou, skip to my Lou; Lou, Lou, skip to my Lou, skip to my Lou, my dar-ling.

The Star-Spangled Banner

Oh,__ say can you see, by the dawn's ear-ly light, What so proud-ly we hailed at the

twi-light's last gleam-ing.

"The Marine's Hymn" is the official song of the United States
Marine Corps. Notice how the many leaps in the melody seem to
suggest an energy that moving by step would not.

The Marine's Hymn

Traditional

Guitar: capo 3

From the halls of Mon-te-zu-ma To the shores of Trip-o-li; ___

___ We_ fight our coun-try's bat - tles In the air, on land, and sea. ___

___ First to fight for right and free - dom And to keep our hon-or clean, ___

___ We are proud to claim the ti - tle of U - nit-ed States Ma - rine. ___

Courtesy of the United States Marine Corps

● And Finally (We Repeat), Notes Repeat

Melody notes can also repeat—just stay where they are. Look at the
way "Old Abram Brown" begins—with a series of nine notes all the
same.

Old Abram Brown

Words from "Tom Tiddler's Ground" by Walter de la Mare   Music by Benjamin Britten

Old   A - bram Brown is   dead and gone, We'll nev - er   see   him   more.

He   used   to   wear   an   old gray coat All   but - toned down be - fore.

© Copyright 1936 by Boosey & Co., Ltd.; Renewed 1963. Reprinted by Permission of Boosey Hawkes, Inc.

ALL STEPS ARE NOT CREATED EQUAL

Look at this drawing of a tone ladder.
Do you see anything peculiar
about the steps?

Did you notice that the distance between
steps 3 and 4 and between 7 and 8 is not
as great as the distance between the
other steps? What kind of ladder is this?
If you tried to climb it, you'd
probably trip!

Actually this is a musical ladder—a scale. Do you remember the one
on page 96? If you play the scale, you might notice that the size of
the steps is not always the same. Some steps are whole steps and
others are half steps. (See the piano keyboard on page 101.) Here is
a scale on E♭ with the whole steps and half steps shown. Play the
whole and half steps to hear their special "sound."

⊔ or ⊓ = whole step   ∨ or ∧ = half step

"Hello, My Baby" uses both whole steps and half steps. You can see
some of the whole and half steps marked. Can you find others?

Hello, My Baby

Words and Music by I. Emerson and J. E. Howard

Guitar: capo 3

If you re-fuse me, hon-ey, you'll lose me, Then you'll be left a-

lone; Oh, ba - by, tel - e - phone and tell me I'm your __

1.
own. Hel - lo! Hel - lo! Hel - lo there!

2.
own! __

● Step to the Piano, Maestro

The piano keyboard is especially handy for showing whole steps and
half steps. Look at this keyboard. Between every white key and
black key there is a half step. But look at notes E and F and notes
B and C. There is no black note separating them. That's because
there is already a natural half step between these notes.

Now look at the **frets** on the fingerboard of this dulcimer.
Can you see that the frets are not the same size?
Some are wider than others. The wider frets
are whole steps and the narrower ones
are half steps.

THE MAJOR SCALE

The pattern of whole steps and half steps in a scale is very important. It gives a scale its special "sound." The scales you have seen so far have all been **major** scales. A major scale has a step pattern of whole, whole, half, whole, whole, whole, half. As long as the pattern is followed, the scale will sound major no matter what note it begins on. That's why "Hello, My Baby" sounded as major as the scale on C. The scale still followed the major-scale pattern, even though it began on E♭.

Scale on E♭

E♭ F G A♭ B♭ C D E♭

Scale on C

C D E F G A B C

Key Signatures

A **key signature** is a kind of shorthand method to tell us what sharps (♯) or flats (♭) are needed to make the scale pattern conform to the whole step-half step pattern. (A sharp raises a note one half step, while a flat lowers it one half step.) Look at the E♭ scale again.

E♭   F   G   A♭   B♭   C   D   E♭

There are three flats needed to make the E♭ scale conform to the major-scale pattern. Since the flatted notes—E♭, A♭, and B♭—will appear each time, musicians simply gather those flats together and place them on the staff at the beginning of the line, like this:

That way the scale can be shown without writing flats all the time.

E♭   F   G   A♭   B♭   C   D   E♭

Here is a song in major key. It is in the key of C major. That means no sharps or flats are needed in the signature. Why is this so?

Merry Minstrels

Attributed to Henry Purcell

Guitar:

We mer - ry min - strels soft mu - sic en - joy, For mu - sic doth ha - tred and mal - ice de - stroy. We sing so blithe - ly, we drive a - way care, And with our soft har - mo - ny ban - ish de - spair. Then hail, _ sweet _ sci - ence, hail, hail, heav'n - ly sound! No plea - sure _ like _ mu - sic on earth can be found.

THE MINOR SCALE

Look at these two scales. The one on the left is a major scale on C.
The one on the right is a **minor** scale, also on C.

C major

C D E F G A B C

C minor

C D Eb F G Ab Bb C

Play the two scales up and down to hear their special sound. What
do you notice about their whole- and half-step patterns? The major-
scale pattern is W W H W W W H. The minor scale, however, has a
pattern of W H W W H W W.

"Hatikvah" is written on a minor scale based on D. It would look
like this. Notice the key signature. We say that this is the key of D
minor.

D E F G A Bb C D

Hatikvah
(Hope)

Hebrew Words by Naftali Herz Imber   English Words by David Eddleman

Traditional Hebrew Melody

Guitar: capo 5

Kol____ od ba - le - vav p' ni ____ - mah   Ne - fesh y' - hu - di
kohl   ohd bah - leh - vahv puh - nee ____ - mah   neh - fehsh yuh - hoo - dee
Yearn - ing for free - dom in Zi - on's ___ land,   Each He - brew soul, by

ho - mi - yah, Ul - fa - 'a - tei ___ miz - rach ka - di - mah,   A - yin l' - tsi - on
hoh - mee - yah ool - fah - 'ah - tay   meez - rahkh kah - dee - mah   ah - yeen luh - tsee - ohn
God's ___ com - mand, Is gaz - ing to the East with shin - ing ___ eyes, Look - ing to Zi - on, the

tso - fi - yah.   Od lo av - dah tik - va - te - nu,   Ha - tik - vah bat
tsoh - fee - yah   ohd loh ahv - dah teek - vah - tay - noo   hah - teek - vah baht
an - cient ___ prize. 'Twas not lost, our hope ___ so ___ sure,   Through the a - ges

CALL CHART 6

Listen to this Call Chart. Some of the selections are in major keys; others are in minor keys.

1. *The Nutcracker,* "Chinese Dance" (excerpt) . . . . Tchaikovsky
2. *L'Arlésienne,* "Prélude" (excerpt) . . . . Bizet
3. *Sinfonietta,* Movement 1 (excerpt) . . . . Janácek
4. *Peer Gynt,* "In the Hall of the Mountain King" (excerpt) . . Grieg
5. *The Water Music,* "Allegro" (excerpt) . . . . Handel

Some songs begin in minor and go to major. This song is one of them. Can you tell when the melody changes to major and when it returns to minor? (You will find this song notated on page 300.)

Time in a Bottle. . . . . Croce

THE PENTATONIC SCALE

The illustration above should give you a clue to the pattern of one of
the most ancient scales still popular today. It has only five notes
and is often heard in folk music from both long ago and now. Many
popular songs also use this scale pattern. Beginning on C, the five-
note scale would look like this.

Have you noticed the gap between E and G? The name given to this
kind of scale is *pentatonic* (*penta-*, 'five'; *tonic-*, 'notes'). Try playing
this scale up and down on bells or piano. Did you notice that there
are no half steps in this scale? That is what gives it its special
sound. Here is another pentatonic scale, this time beginning on G.

You can create pentatonic scales starting from any note. All will
share the same special sound, and are great for inventing good
melodies.

In this song the first part of the melody, marked A, is based on the pentatonic scale you just played. The second part, marked B, goes to the major scale, but it uses only *five* of the notes of the major scale—F#, G, A, B, and C. That way there is a five-note correspondence between section A and section B. Can you hear the difference as you sing?

I'd Like to Teach the World to Sing

Words and Music by Bill Backer, Billy Davis, Roger Cook and Roger Greenaway
Arranged by David Fiorenza and Daniel Shigo

I'd like to teach the world to sing____ in
I'd like to build the world a home__ and
I'd like to see the world for once__ all

per - fect har - mo - ny.____ I'd like to hold it
fur - nish it with love, ____ Grow ap - ple trees and
stand - ing hand in hand, ____ And hear them e - cho

in my arms__ and keep it com - pa - ny.____
hon - ey bees__ and snow - white tur - tle doves.____
through the hills__ for peace through - out the land.____

That's the song I hear, Let the world sing to -
That's the song I hear,

day.____ A song of peace that
Let the world sing to - day.

D.C. al Fine—first line only

e - choes on ____ and nev - er goes a - way.____

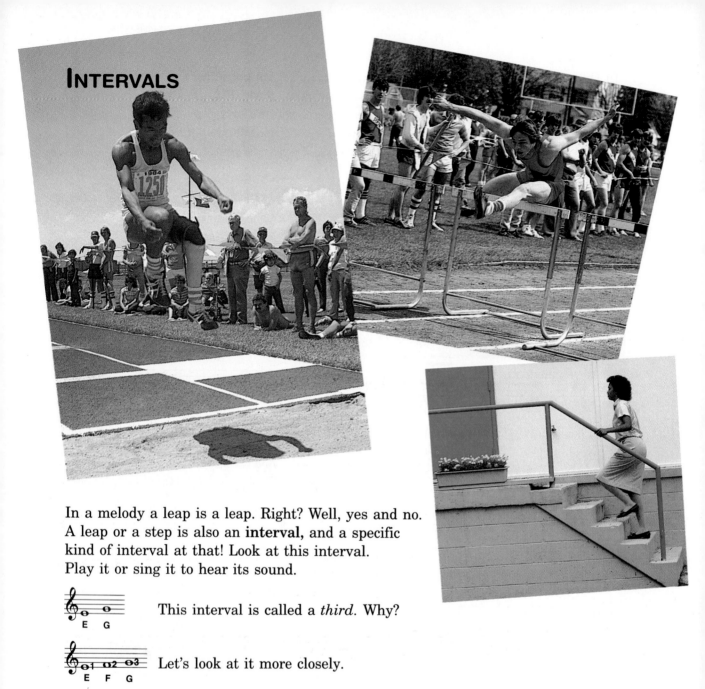

INTERVALS

In a melody a leap is a leap. Right? Well, yes and no.
A leap or a step is also an **interval,** and a specific
kind of interval at that! Look at this interval.
Play it or sing it to hear its sound.

This interval is called a *third*. Why?

E G

Let's look at it more closely.

E F G

If you start with the lower note of the interval and count up by *lines and
spaces* to the higher note, the number you place on the higher note
will tell you its interval—in this case, a third. Look at these intervals.
Can you tell what they are by counting the lines and spaces?

On page 109 the song "You're Never Fully Dressed Without a Smile"
contains many intervals of different widths. Can you name the
intervals in the boxes?

You're Never Fully Dressed Without a Smile

from *Annie*

Words by Martin Charnin   Music by Charles Strouse

Hey, ho - bo man, Hey, Dap - per Dan, You both__ got your
Your clothes__ may be Beau Brum - el - ly, They stand__ out a

style,}
mile,} But bro - ther, You're nev - er ful - ly____ dressed with - out a

smile!_____   smile!_____ Who cares what they're

wear - ing on Main Street or Sa - vile Row? It's what you wear from ear to

ear, and not from head to toe that mat - ters; So, Sen - a - tor,

So, jan - i - tor, So long__ for a while, Re - mem - ber, you're

nev - er ful - ly____ dressed, though you may wear the__ best, You're

nev - er ful - ly dressed with - out a smile._____

MELODY—ON ITS CONSTRUCTION SITE

What have you discovered so far? You have discovered that composers have quite a few melodic devices to help them build a melody. One was *repetition*. Listen to how these composers use repetition of phrases, motives, or notes to build a melody.

Melody Building

The Olympian (excerpt) . . . . Glass

Carmina Burana, "O Fortuna" (excerpt) . . . . Orff

Symphony No. 7 in A, Movement 2 (excerpt) . . Beethoven

What kind of repetition does the composer use in this song?

Just in Time

from *Bells Are Ringing*

Words by Betty Comden and Adolph Green   Music by Jule Styne

Guitar: capo 3

Just in time, __ I found you just in time. __ Be-fore you came, my time __ was run-ning low. __ I was lost, __ The los-ing dice were tossed, __ My bridg-es all were crossed, __ No-where to go. __ Now you're here __ and now I know just where I'm go - ing, no more doubt or fear, __ I've found my way. __ For love came just in time. __ You found me just in time __ And changed my lone-ly life that love - ly day. __

● Sequence

Do you know what a sequence is? You probably know that a sequence is a series of events or objects. In music, **sequence** has a very precise meaning. Look at this melodic example.

The first measure is a simple melodic idea called a **motive.** The next two measures have exactly the same pattern except that each one begins a step lower. That's a sequence, and it's a good tool for composers when they need to expand their material.

This song has many sequences. After you've learned to sing it, can you discover if <u>all</u> the sequences begin one step lower than the motive?

VARIATION AND CONTRAST

The apples in the picture represent
a wide variety of this common fruit.
The oranges, on the other hand,
are a contrast to the apples.
Oranges are quite different
from apples.

Composers use **variation** and contrast to make their melodies
interesting. Look at the melody of "This Old Hammer." See how the
many melodic devices, including variation and contrast, make this
melody "work."

● Add Rhythm to Move a Melody

Do you remember *Gaudeamus omnes in Domino* on page 70? It was an example of medieval plainsong and seemed to have no regular rhythm. The rhythm was created by the words. Every melody—even a seemingly nonrhythmic one like *Gaudeamus*—needs rhythm to give it shape and character. Look at this four-note motive, for example.

E   F♯   G♯   A

Now add rhythm and see what happens.

"One of Those Songs"   **"Chester"**

Look at "Row, Row, Row Your Boat." This simple round that you have probably sung all your life takes on a whole new character when the rhythm is changed.

Row, Row, Row Your Boat

Traditional Round

Row,   row,   row   your boat   Gen - tly down   the   stream; ___

Mer - ri - ly, mer - ri - ly,   mer - ri - ly, mer - ri - ly,   Life   is but   a   dream. __

CLAP A RHYTHM, CALL A SONG!

On page 113 you saw a four-note motive combined with two rhythm patterns that helped identify two songs from your book. Now here is a short rhythm pattern. Can you name any songs that use this rhythm?

Redwood trees

Now for the big event! Combine the rhythm pattern above with the note pattern on page 113 and sing . . .

This Land Is Your Land

Words and Music by Woody Guthrie   Countermelody by Ruth Tutelman

REFRAIN
Countermelody (sing last time only)

Guitar: capo 3

This land   is   your   land,   this land   is
This land   is   your   land, ____   this land   is   my   land, ____
mine,   From   Maine to   Mon - ta   - na,   des - ert   to the
____ From Cal - i - for - nia _____   to the New York   is - land; ____

TRO—© copyright 1956 (renewed 1984), 1958 (renewed 1986) and 1970 Ludlow Music, Inc., New York, N.Y. Used by permission.

shore, We sing that this land is your land, this land is

_ From the red-wood for - est _____ to the Gulf Stream wa - ters; _

mine, Yes, it's made for you and me. _____

_ This land was made for you and me. _____

VERSE

1. As I was walk - ing _____ that rib - bon of high - way, _
2. I've roamed and ram - bled _____ and I fol-lowed my foot - steps _
3. When the sun comes shin - ing _____ and I _ was stroll - ing _

_ I saw a - bove me _____ that end - less sky - way, _
_ to the spar - kling sands of _____ her dia - mond des - erts, _
_ And the wheat-fields wav - ing _____ and the dust clouds roll - ing, _

_ I saw be - low me _____ that gold - en val - ley, _
_ And all a - round me _____ a voice was sound - ing, _
_ As the fog was lift - ing _____ a voice was chant - ing, _

_ This land was made for you and me. _____
_ "This land was made for you and me." _____
_ "This land was made for you and me." _____

BEATS IN GROUPS

● Meter in 2

What do you notice about these quarter notes? ♩ ♩ ♩ ♩

There isn't much to notice is there? They're just plodding along.
But what happens when we **accent** (>) every other one?

♩ ♩ ♩ ♩
>   >

The beats are grouped in *twos*—a **meter** *in 2*. Musicians usually put
bar lines between each grouping: ♩ ♩ |♩ ♩ |

Look at the conducting pattern in $\frac{2}{4}$ meter.
Try conducting some songs in this book
that are in a meter of 2.

● The Meter Signature

A meter needs a meter signature to tell the musicians what the
meter grouping is and what note is going to represent the beat. The
bottom number of the meter signature tells you what kind of note
represents the beat; so $\frac{2}{8}$ means that the eighth note (♪) represents
the beat and $\frac{2}{2}$ means that the half note (♩) represents the beat and
$\frac{2}{4}$ means that the quarter note (♩) represents the beat. The key idea,
however, is that if there is a top number 2, the meter is in 2 no
matter what note represents the beat.

● Meter in 4

Many songs in this book are in a meter of 4. They carry a meter
signature of $\frac{4}{4}$. That means the beats are grouped in fours and a
quarter note (♩) represents the beat. Look at the conducting pattern
for a meter of 4.

On page 117 is a song in $\frac{4}{4}$ meter. Learn the conducting patterns and
conduct that song or any other songs in meter of 4 in your book.

The Rose

Words and Music by Amanda McBroom

Guitar: capo 5

1. Some say love, it is a riv - er that drowns ___ the ten - der ___ reed.

Some say love, it is a raz - or that leaves ___ your soul to ___ bleed.

Some say ___ love, ___ it is a hun - ger, an end - less ach - ing need. ___

I say ___ love, it is a flow - er, and you it's on - ly seed. ___

2. It's the ___ heart a - fraid of break - in' that nev - er ___ learns to ___ dance.
3. When the ___ night has been too lone - ly, and the road ___ has been too ___ long,

It's the ___ dream ___ a-fraid of wak - in' that nev - er ___ takes the ___ chance.
And you ___ think ___ that love is on - ly for the luck-y ___ and the ___ strong,

It's the ___ one ___ who won't be tak-en ___ who can - not seem to give, ___
Just re - mem - ber, ___ in ___ the win - ter, ___ far be - neath ___ the win - ter snows ___

1.
And the ___ soul a - fraid of dy - in', that nev-er ___ learns to live. ___
Lies the ___ seed that with the sun's ___ love, in the

2.
spring be - comes the rose. ___

● Meter in 3

Listen to these recordings of waltzes. Can you feel that the beats are grouped in threes?

Belle of the Ball (excerpt) .... Anderson
Masquerade Suite, "Waltz" (excerpt) .... Khachaturian

Look at the way these quarter notes are now grouped in threes.

And if we place bar lines in the right places and add an appropriate meter signature, we are ready to conduct in 3!

Look at the conducting pattern below. Try it out. It will help you feel the meter in 3. When you think you have practiced the conducting pattern for 3 enough, try conducting the song that begins below.

My White Horse
(Mi caballo blanco)

Guitar: capo 2   Words and Music by Francisco Flores del Campo   English Words by Samuele Maquí

My horse is like the sun - rise, —   My horse as white as dawn.
Es mi ca - ba - llo blan - co, —   Co - moun a - ma - ne - cer,
ehs mee cah-bah-yoh blahn - koh   coh-mohoon ah-mah-neh - sehr

We al - ways ride to - geth - er —   Sing - ing as we ride a - long.
Siem - pre jun - ti - tos va - mos, _   Es mia - mi - go mas fi - el.
syehm-preh hoon-tee-tohs vah - mohs   ehs meehah-mee-goh mahs fee - ehl

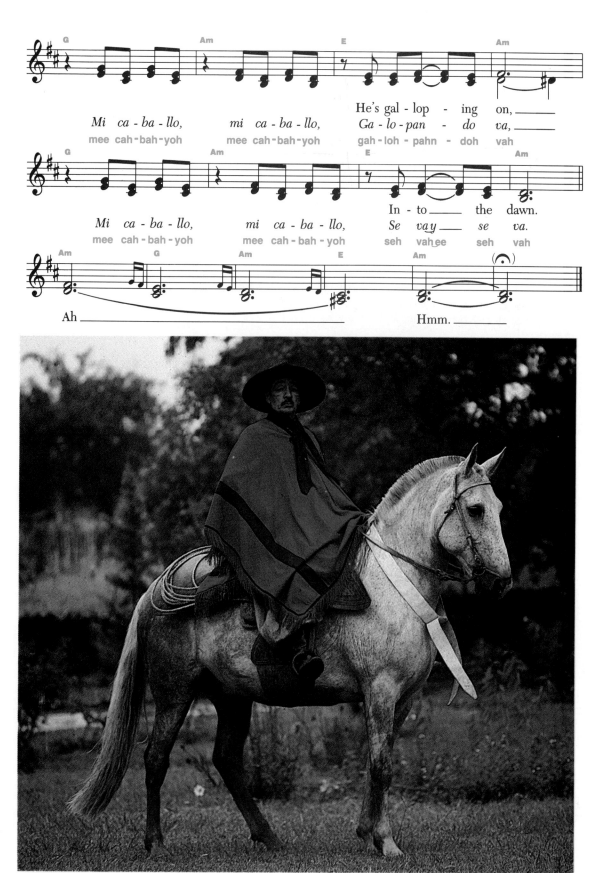

Mi ca - ba - llo,   *mi ca - ba - llo,*   He's gal - lop - ing on, _____
mee cah‑bah‑yoh   mee cah‑bah‑yoh   *Ga - lo - pan - do va,* _____
gah - loh - pahn - doh vah

Mi ca - ba - llo,   *mi ca - ba - llo,*   In - to _____ the dawn.
mee cah‑bah‑yoh   mee cah‑bah‑yoh   *Se vay _____ se va.*
seh vah ee seh vah

Ah _____ Hmm. _____

A South American gaucho (cowboy)

Alternating 2 and 3 (A Neat Trick)

Many composers, especially those of the twentieth century, have been attracted to **multimeter,** a verbal mouthful that simply means "more than one meter in a composition." In this setting of "Tumbalalaika," the arranger has taken an old folk song and altered its meter to give it an unusual feeling. Notice that the first few measures are in $\frac{3}{4}$, and the *Tumbalalaika* words are set in $\frac{2}{2}$. Verse 4 (on page 121) is the tricky part. Look at its meter signature. It is $\frac{3}{4}\frac{2}{4}$. That means the metric grouping changes with each measure—from $\frac{3}{4}$ to $\frac{2}{4}$ and back again.

Tumbalalaika

Jewish Folk Song   English Words by Margaret Fishback   Arranged by Lawrence Eisman

Tum - bal - a, tum - bal - a, tum - bal - a - lai - ka.

Tum - bal - a - lai - ka, play bal - a - lai - ka,

Tum - bal - a - lai - ka, laugh as you play.

4. Tum - bal - a, Tum - bal, Tum - bal - a - lai - ka,

Tum - bal - a, Tum - bal, Tum - bal - a - lai - ka,

Tum - bal - a - lai - ka, play bal - a - lai - ka,

Tum - bal - a - lai - ka, laugh as you play.

THE LONG AND THE SHORT OF IT

Sooner or later the time comes to talk seriously about notation. You may have had some study in musical notation before now, perhaps in a lower school grade; in band, orchestra, or chorus; or in private lessons. It is very hard to talk about music if you don't know at least the basics of notation. Here goes.

Basically, notes show how long they are to be held. They don't even need a staff to do that. When notes are introduced on a staff, their placement shows the *pitch* of the notes. (But you probably already know that.)

If you can divide by two, you can understand rhythm notation. The largest unit of rhythm notation is the *whole note*: o

The whole note (o) and every smaller note can be divided in half. So the whole note can be broken into two halves: o = ♩ ♩

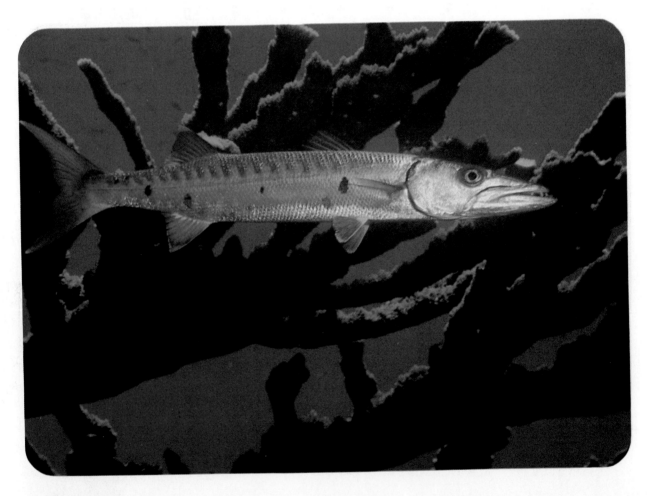

And breaking down further we find . . .

Do you notice how each note is named for its division from the whole note? That helps to figure out its relationship to all other notes.

MUSIC'S TRIPLE THREAT—THE TRIPLET

Do you see anything unusual in this song from *Oliver*? Follow it as
you listen to the recording.

***Oliver!*, "Food, Glorious Food" (excerpt)** .... **Bart**

Food, glo - ri - ous food! Hot sau - sage and mus - tard; While we're in the mood,

Cold jel - ly and cus - tard! Pease, pud - ding and sa - ve - loys, "What next?" is the ques - tion.

Rich gen - tle - men have it, boys: In - dye - ges - tion!

If you heard the rhythm ♩♩♩, you heard a **triplet**. Triplets are
three equal notes spread over the space of two of the same value.
Try clapping this rhythm to get the feel of triplets. It's simple! (The
numbers in red show the steady beat.)

1 2 3 4 1 2 3 4 1 2 3 4 1 2 3 4

⬤ And What Does That Little Dot Do?

That little dot that you often see after a note simply makes the note
last longer by half its value. For example, if the note is a quarter
note (♩), a dot added (♩.) gives it the value of a quarter note and an
eighth note (♩‿♪). Look at the eighth notes and dotted quarter
notes in the song above. You will see them in measures 2, 4, 6, and
8. The combination of these two notes (♪ ♩.) makes up a length of
four eighth notes (♪ ♪. ♪ ♪).

MORE ON SYNCOPATION

You learned on page 20 what syncopation is. It's a kind of shifting of emphasis of the beat. Sometimes, musicians will speak of syncopation as "playing on the offbeat." This American ragtime "classic" by Scott Joplin was written about the turn of the twentieth century. Listen for the syncopation—the off beats—especially the ones that look like this:

The Entertainer . . . . Joplin

Scott Joplin

Here's another piece for piano. Notice how this composer uses the same syncopated pattern. Is there any difference in the feeling?

Pasquinade, "Caprice". . . . . Gottschalk

It's fun to take some "square rhythm" songs and "jazz them up" with syncopation. Try singing this jazz version of *Row, Row, Row Your Boat.*

Row, Row, Row Your Boat (jazz version)

PLAYING ALONG

Now that you know something about rhythm, learn to sing this
song, and then add a rhythm accompaniment to it.

I'm an Old Cowhand

Words and Music by Johnny Mercer

Guitar: capo 3

1. I'm an old cow - hand ____ from the Ri - o Grande, ____ But my legs ain't bowed ____
2. I'm an old cow - hand ____ from the Ri - o Grande, ____ And I learned to ride ____

____ and my face ain't tanned, ____ I'm a cow-boy who nev-er saw a cow, Nev-er
____ 'fore I learned to stand, ____ I'm a rid - in' fool who is up to date, I know

roped a steer, 'cause I don't know how, And I sho' ain't fix - in' to start in now.
ev - 'ry trail in the Lone Star State, 'Cause I ride the trail in a big V - Eight.

Yip-py - I - O - Ki - Ay, ____ Yip-py - I - O - Ki - Ay Ay. ____

3. I'm an old cowhand
   From the Rio Grande,
   And I come to town
   Just to hear the band,
   I know all the songs that the cowboys know,
   'Bout the big corral where the dogies go,
   'Cause I learned them all on the radio.
   Yippy-I-O-Ki-Ay . . .

4. I'm an old cowhand
   From the Rio Grande,
   Where the West is wild,
   'Round the Borderland,
   Where the buffalo roam around the zoo,
   And the good folks make you a rug or two,
   And the old Bar X is a Bar-B-Q.
   Yippy-I-O-Ki-Ay . . .

And now add some or all of these rhythm parts. If you don't have
the instruments called for here, use any substitute.

TEMPO

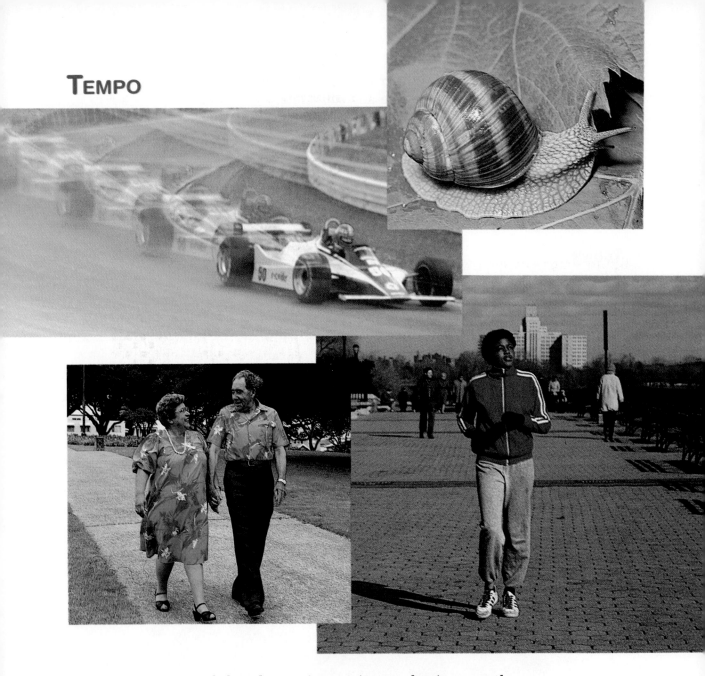

Have you ever noticed that the music you sing or play is never the same speed? Sometimes it's slow, sometimes fast. Sometimes it's right in between. The speed of a piece of music, whether slow or fast, is called *tempo*. Often, composers will try to tell performers how fast or slow to perform their music. They will sometimes use Italian words. Here are some of the terms composers might use.

Presto—very fast

Allegro—lively

Moderato—moderate

Andante—walking tempo

Adagio—slow

Largo—very slow

Which of those words might you choose to describe the pictures above?

The problem with the Italian words on page 128 is that they mean different things to different people. Your interpretation of "very fast" may be quite different from that of your classmate's, whose "very fast" may not be nearly as fast as yours. This is one reason why a piece of music may be performed in so many different ways; the performer must bring his or her own sense of tempo to it.

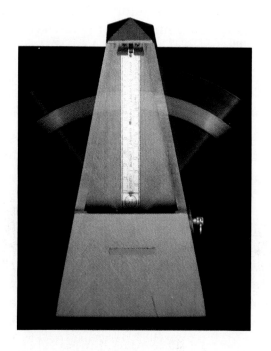

Some composers have tried to be more precise about the tempos they want. They often use a machine called a **metronome,** which was first used extensively by Beethoven. It establishes an unwavering beat at just the tempo the composer wants. Music, however, is not a precise art, and the metronome, while useful, has not answered the question, What is the perfect tempo for a particular piece of music?

Tempo can also change within a space of time. This can often be clearly heard in spoken dialogue. Listen to this brief exchange from an imaginary radio show. You can hear the speeding up and slowing down of the dialogue.

"Sherlock Holmes" Scene

Composers sometimes exploit the concept of getting faster and getting slower just for its own sake. Listen to this well-known composition by Brazilian composer Heitor Villa-Lobos (HAY tohr veel lah LOH bohsh). His musical description of a train getting faster (*accelerando*) (ah chehl eh RAHN doh) and slowing down (*ritardando*) (ree tahr DAHN doh) has become a favorite of concertgoers all over the world.

The Little Train of the Caipira . . . . Villa-Lobos

HARMONY—GETTING IT ALL TOGETHER

Do you remember the harmony from the Middle Ages? You read about it on page 73 and listened to an example of it. Basically it was a melody duplicated, or doubled, at another interval, usually the fifth or the fourth interval below the melody. In this example of "Row, Row, Row Your Boat," the melody is harmonized at the fourth below. (The example is in the key of G to keep it on the staff.)

Row, row, row your boat, gent-ly down the stream, _

Mer-ri - ly, mer-ri - ly, mer-ri - ly, mer-ri - ly, Life is but a dream. _

While doubling of melodies began with the intervals of the fourth and fifth, the third and the sixth eventually prevailed as the intervals of choice. In some countries, such as Mexico, the use of the third as a harmonizing interval is almost a national musical characteristic. Learn to sing this song from Mexico and work out the harmonization in thirds. When you have learned it, try doubling the melody a fourth below. How does the feeling of the song change?

De colores

Guitar: capo 3   Mexican Folk Song   English Words by Alice Firgau and Samuele Maqui

1. De _____ co - lo - res, _____ De co - lo - res se vis - ten los cam - pos en
   deh   koh - loh - rehs   deh koh - loh - rehs seh vees-tehn lohs cahm-pohs ehn
   When _____ the mead - ows, _____ when the mead-ows burst forth in the cool dew - y

la pri - ma - ve - ra, _____ De _____ co -
lah pree - mah - veh - rah   deh   koh -
col - ors of spring - time; _____ When _____ the

lo - res, ___ De co - lo - res son los pa - ja - ri - tos que vie - nen dea
loh - rehs deh koh - loh - rehs sohn lohs pah - hah - ree - tohs keh vee-eh-nehn deh-ah
swal - lows, ___ when the swal-lows come wing-ing in clouds of bright col - ors from

fue - ra, ___ De co - lo - res, ___
fooeh - rah deh koh - loh - rehs
far off; ___ When ___ the rain - bow, ___

___ De co - lo - res es el ar - co i - ris que ve - mos lu - cir, ___
deh koh - loh - rehs ehs ehl ahr - coh ee - reehs keh veh-mohs loo - seer
___ when the rain-bow spreads rib-bons of col - or all o - ver the sky, ___

Y por e - so los gran - des a - mo - res de mu - chos co - lo - res me
ee pohr eh - soh lohs grahn-dehs ah - moh-rehs deh moo-chohs koh - loh-rehs meh
Then I know why the splen-dors of true love are great and their col - ors, the

gus - tan a mi. ___ gus - tan a mi. ___
goos - tahn ah mee goos - tahn ah mee
best ones of all. ___ best ones of all. ___

De Colores, traditional, arranged, and adapted by Joan Baez © 1974, Chandos Music. (ASCAP)

2. Canta el gallo, Canta el gallo con el
   quiri quiri quiri quiri quiri;
   La gallina, La gallina con el
   cara cara cara cara cara;
   Los polluelos, Los polluelos con el
   pio pio pio pio pi,
   Y por eso los grandes amores de muchos
   colores me gustan a mi. *(2 times)*

kahn-tah eh gah-yoh kahn-tah eh gah-yo kohn ehl
   kee-ree kee-ree kee-ree kee-ree kee-ree
lah gah-yee-na lah gah-yee-na kohn ehl
   kah-rah kah-rah kah-rah kah-rah kah-rah
lohs poh-yweh-lohs lohs poh-yweh-lohs kohn ehl
   pee-oh pee-oh pee-oh pee-oh pee
ee pohr eh-soh lohs grahn-dehs ah-moh-rehs deh moo-chohs
   koh-loh-rehs meh goos-tahn ah mee *(2 times)*

Hear the rooster, Hear the rooster that calls
   quiri quiri quiri quiri quiri,
Hear his lady, Hear his lady sing back
   cara cara cara cara cara,
Hear the small ones, Hear the small ones call out
   pio pio pio pio pi,
And my favorite folks are the folks who wear colors,
   the colors so pleasant to me. (2 times)

Harmony, Harmony, Quite Contrary

Harmonizing a melody does not always mean moving in parallel motion. Sometimes, harmony parts may also move in an opposite direction from that of the melody line. This kind of contrary motion can provide more variety in a piece. Here is a song you may have sung many times at camp. Listen for the way the **countermelody** works as a mirror image of the melody at the beginning of the first three phrases.

Tell Me Why

Traditional

Countermelody (2nd verse only)

2. Be - cause God made ___ the stars to shine,

1. Tell ___ me why ___ the stars do shine,
2. Be - cause God made ___ the stars to shine,

Be - cause God made ___ the i - vy twine,

Tell ___ me why ___ the i - vy twines, Then
Be - cause God made ___ the i - vy twine,

Be - cause God made ___ the sky so blue,

tell ___ me why ___ the sky is blue,
Be - cause God made ___ the sky so blue,

Be - cause God made you so sweet ___ and true.

And I will tell you why I ___ love you.
Be - cause God made you so sweet ___ and true.

POLYPHONIC TEXTURE

On page 73 you learned what polyphonic texture is. It is two or more voices singing independent vocal lines. A canon, or a round, can be a good example of polyphonic texture. (But be careful. Some rounds are really homophonic—all voices singing different notes but moving in the same rhythm.) This round is a good representation of the polyphonic round. If you examine each line, you will see that each one is different in melodic direction and rhythm.

A Home on the Rolling Sea

Words and Music by David Eddleman

I
Give me a home on the roll - ing sea, and let me be a sail - or;

II
Let me_____ a sail - or be;

III
Let me sail off on a ship for a life on the rol - lick - ing sea.

● The Fugue—A Flighty Form that Always Has an Answer

While the round may be the simplest imitative form, the **fugue** (FYOOG), from the Italian word *fuga*, meaning "flight," can be the most complex. The fugue begins like a canon, but it adds other lines and parts, including some sections that may be only bits and pieces of what has gone before. Often the fugue will end with a stretto (STREHT toh), in which the subject—the melody—enters rapidly, overlapping the other voices very quickly.

Listen to this fugue by J.S. Bach. Can you hear the subject entering and reentering? When you have heard it, you may want to play the short fugue on page 134. It contains all the parts of a fugue. Try playing it on recorders with your classmates.

LISTENING LIBRARY

Fugue in D Minor.................................Bach

Fugue in G

David Eddleman

TIE THE MUSIC UP WITH CHORDS

Triads, the most common chords, come from the scale that the melody is based on. A triad can be built on any scale tone just by adding thirds, like these triads in G major.

For "Ode to Joy" you will need three chords—the G-major (G, B and D), D-major (D, F♯, and A), and A-major (A, C♯, and E). Play even quarter notes on piano or bells, changing chords with the chord symbol over the music.

Henry van Dyke, "Hymn of Joy" from the Poems of Henry van Dyke. Reprinted with the permission of Charles Scribner's Sons.

Tone Color—The Sounds of Music

Noise

I like noise.
The wh*oo*p of a boy, the thu*d* of a hoof,
The ra*ttl*e of rain on a galvanized roof,
The hu*bbub* of traffic, the r*oar* of a train,
The *throb* of machinery n*um*bing the brain,
The *switch*ing of wires in an overhead tram.
The r*ush* of the wind, a door on the slam.
The boom of the thunder, the *crash* of the waves,
The din of a river that *races* and *raves*,
The *crack* of a rifle, the *clank* of a pail,
The strident tattoo of a *swift-slapp*ing sail.
From any old sound that the sile*nce* destroys
Arises a gamut of soul-stirring joys.
I like noise.

J. Pope
© PUNCH London

 Collage of Sounds

The collage of sounds you heard was a mixture of the sounds produced by objects all around. Could you tell them apart? If you could tell what the sounds were, you were identifying their **tone color**—the way they sound. The rain has a "rain color," the car horn has a "car horn color," the train has a "train color," and so on.

● Colors of the Night

Composers use tone color to add to the expression of their music
just as painters use the colors of the spectrum to create and
enhance feeling in their paintings. Look at the reproduction of
Vincent van Gogh's (van GOH) famous painting *The Starry Night*. It
is a night scene, yet there is a torrent of color—oranges, blues,
yellows, even whites. The swirls of color around the haloed stars are
reflected in the swirls of blue and purple in the hills in the
background. The feeling is that of motion within stillness, power
within calm. Could van Gogh have achieved these feelings and
effects in any other way or with other colors? It makes no difference,
really. The work stands as a piece unique in itself, forming its own
character from the painter's colors and shapes.

THE STARRY NIGHT   *Vincent van Gogh*

Vincent van Gogh,
The Starry Night, The Museum of Modern Art, New York. Collection, Acquired through the Lillie P. Bliss Bequest.

SING THOSE GOLDEN TONES

Patti LaBelle

Plácido Domingo

Louis Armstrong

Lena Horne

Barbra Streisand

Voices, too, vary widely in their sound and quality. Barbra Streisand's voice does not have the same tone color as Lena Horne's, and both voices are quite unlike Patti LaBelle's. Plácido Domingo's voice is big and brilliant and filled with the kind of grand-opera tone quality we would expect. Louis Armstrong's distinctive "laryngitis" sound is immediately recognizable to almost everyone. With singers, individual tone color is part of their trademark. When someone hears a new recording by one of these artists, it is important to the singer that he or she be recognizable, even though no announcement has been made about the performer's identity.

Listen to two vocalists perform "Send In the Clowns" from *A Little Night Music*. Can you hear how the quality and color of each voice changes the expression of the song?

A Little Night Music, "Send In the Clowns" . . . . Sondheim
1. Judy Collins, vocalist
2. Lisa Skiba, vocalist

● Three Performers, One Piece

Even the same instrumental piece can sound different in the hands of different performers. Listen to these three performances of Chopin's *Waltz in C♯ Minor*. What differences can you hear in them?

Waltz in C♯ Minor (excerpt) . . . . Chopin
1. Dinu Lipatti, pianist
2. Arthur Rubinstein, pianist
3. Philippe Entremont, pianist

● Some Singers Do It All

Today there is a singer who is combining the career of a rock singer with that of an opera singer. Listen to two recordings of Peter Hofmann, a young German tenor, as he shows off his ability to be both "serious" and "popular."

Die Walküre, "Winterstürme" . . . . Wagner

Peter Hofmann

The Long and Winding Road . . . . Lennon/McCartney

INSTRUMENTAL MUSIC'S FOUR BASIC COLORS

You know that the color spectrum consists of three primary colors—red, yellow, and blue. All other colors are made by combining these three colors in many different ways.

Music has color, too. In addition to the various vocal colors, instruments fall into four basic color categories. Look at these pictures and listen to some music specially written for each group.

The Brass

Brass Quartet "In Honorem Paul Hindemith," Movement 1 . . . . Eddleman

The Woodwinds

La cheminée du Roi René, Movement 1. . . . . Milhaud

The Strings

Adagio for Strings . . . . Barber

The Percussion

The Aztec Gods, Movement 1 . . . . Read

● How's Your Color Sense?

Composers, when they write for instruments, usually have a particular set of instruments in mind for their compositions. *Tales from the Latin Woods* is just such a piece. The composer had a very specific set of tone colors in mind for this piece, and each part can be most easily played by the instrument for which he wrote it.

Listen to *Tales from the Latin Woods* as played by each of the four instrumental groups. Then decide which group sounds most appropriate. Don't worry if you guess wrong! Music is an art, not a science, and you may very well hear the brass, woodwinds, strings, or percussion as more appropriate than the composer's solution. The composer won't mind!

Tales from the Latin Woods .... Eddleman
1. Brass group
2. String group
3. Woodwind group
4. Percussion group

CALL CHART 7

Listen to the way one composer put all the instrumental colors together in "Russian Sailor's Dance." The Call Chart will help you recognize the instruments.

The Red Poppy, "Russian Sailor's Dance" .... Glière

1. Introduction—full orchestra; *ff;* fast
2. Low strings, low brass; *f,* then *mf;* slow
3. Clarinet, strings, tambourine; *mp;* slow
4. Clarinet and piccolo solos, strings accompany; *mf;* slow
5. Horns, woodwinds, tambourine; *f;* fast
6. Strings, tambourine, brass; *ff;* slow
7. Oboe, clarinet, low strings pizzicato (plucked); *mp;* slow
8. Woodwinds, strings, brass, percussion; *ff;* very fast
9. Full orchestra, brass section predominates; *ff;* fast
10. Full orchestra to end; brass drum "stinger"

PATTERNS IN SOUND

Habitat (Montreal, Canada)

Sounds have patterns. Listen to this group of sounds from the world you live in.

Collage of Environmental Sounds

There are patterns in music, as well. All your favorite songs are built on different melody and rhythm patterns that repeat in different ways. They help to make the song sound "logical," as if it all belongs together. This song has a number of patterns. Can you find them?

Scatterbox

Words and Music by Steven L. Rosenhaus

1. I don't need words to sing a song, I can go on all day.
2. Make it all up as you go a-long, you don't e-ven need to rhyme,

And if you want you can sing a-long, Just lis-ten to me and re-peat what I say:
And if it swings you can say that you are hav-ing a mar-ve-lous, won-der-ful time!

TEAM UP WITH YOUR PATTERN

Can you make rhythm patterns out of your name and your friends'

names? *David,* for example, becomes

and *Carolyn* would be . Try making up rhythm

patterns with your classmates' names and chant them together.

Here is a chant ensemble based on the names of well-known football
teams. First clap the patterns, then chant the names.

Now try chanting the
"football team pattern"
with this recording.

Dooji-Wooji . . . . Ellington

LAYERS OF PATTERNS

Have you ever heard a Latin American instrumental group playing *salsa? Salsa* is a Spanish word meaning "sauce" and in this case, it's *hot* sauce. The excitement you may feel when hearing salsa or any other Latin style is often created by the layering of melody and rhythm patterns that repeat over and over, usually with an improvised instrumental or vocal solo on top. (Do you remember the African rhythm complex on page 10?)

Look at this melodic-rhythmic ostinato pattern. First learn to sing it by itself, then add this extra "layer" to the recording of *Do the Mambo.*

Dance to — the rhy - thm, — Come dance to — the rhy - thm, — Come

 Do the Mambo . . . . Eisman/Carr

Composers have used ostinatos for centuries as a way to hold a piece together. Often they weave many variations above and around the ostinato. Here is a piece in which the composer does just that. The ostinato looks like this.

Play it on the piano or on a bass-clef instrument. Then listen to it with the variations.

 ***The Bells of St. Geneviève* (excerpt)**. . . . . Marais

A COMPOSER'S BEST FRIEND IS HIS PATTERN

Composers who use electronic instruments to create their works often use the same devices as do composers who use **acoustical** (ah коо stih kl) means—natural sound. Ostinato, for example, is still a favorite device of the electronic composer, as it is with the acoustical composer. Edward Smaldone has created a short piece for synthesizer using many different patterns. Try to hear how he organizes those patterns.

Piece for Synthesizer ....Smaldone

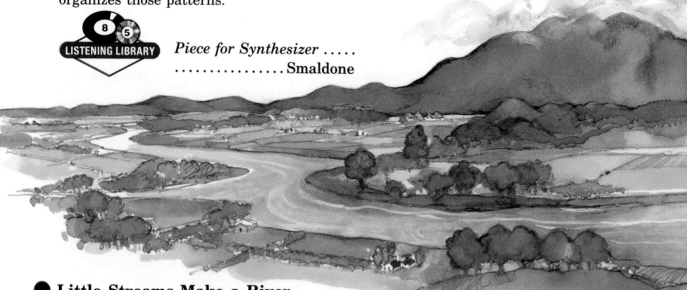

● Little Streams Make a River

Look at the melody and rhythm patterns below. Sing them or play them on any instrument that has the proper range. They are the patterns for most of the accompaniment of *River,* on page 147. Follow the lyric as you listen. When one of these patterns appears, its letter will be written at the appropriate place.

River

Eugene McDaniels

Introduction: A and B

A and B There's a river somewhere,
Flows through the lives of everyone;
And it flows through the valleys and the mountains
   and the meadows of time.

There's a star in the sky,
Brightenin' the lives of everyone;
I know it brightens the valleys and the mountains
   and the meadows of time.
Yes, it do.

Free improvisation *Chorus*: Yes, it do.
There's a voice from the past
A and C Speaks through the lives of everyone;
I know it speaks through the valleys and the mountains
A and C   and the meadows of time.

There's a smile in your eye
A and C Brightens the lives of everyone;
I know it brightens the valleys and the mountains
A and C   and the meadows of time.
Yes, it do.

Free improvisation *Chorus*: Yes, it do.
with A and C

There's a short song of love
C and D Sings through the lives of everyone;
And it sings through the valleys and the mountains
C and D   and the meadows of time.

There's a sweet song of love
C That sings through the lives of everyone;
I know it sings through the valleys and the mountains
C   and the meadows of time.
Free improvisation Yes, it do.

Chorus: Yes, it do.

There's a river somewhere,
D Flows through the lives of everyone;
I know it flows through the valleys and the mountains
C and D   and the meadows of time.

There's a sweet song of love
C Sweetenin' the lives of everyone;
And it sweetens the valleys and the mountains
C   and the meadows of time.
Free improvisation Yes, it do.

Chorus: Yes, it do.

PATTERNS FOR PLAYING
This Old Hammer

Guitar: capo 5

African-American Work Song

1. This old ham-mer _____ killed John Hen-ry, _____ This old
2. Take this ham-mer _____ to the walk-in' boss, _____ Take this

ham-mer _____ killed John Hen-ry, _____ This old ham-mer _____
ham-mer _____ to the walk-in' boss, _____ Take this ham-mer _____

_____ killed John Hen-ry, _____ but it won't kill me, _____
to the walk-in' boss, _____ Tell __ him I'm gone, _____

__ no, it won't __ kill me. _____
__ Oh, _____ tell him I'm gone. _____

Try accompanying "This Old Hammer" using bells. First line up the bells like this.

D minor   G minor   A₇

Here is the chord pattern: D min. | A₇ | D min. | D min. | G min. | A₇ | D min. | D min. | Try playing the chord pattern on bells, using equal quarter notes in each measure: ♩ ♩ ♩ ♩. Then try a more complicated rhythm, such as ♪♩ ♪♩ ♩ or ♩ ♫♫ ♩ or perhaps ♫♫♫ ♩. (Do you remember the name for this type of rhythm?—it's syncopation!) There are numerous combinations you can try. Write your rhythm patterns on the board. When you have enough of them, try layering them as in *River* or the African rhythm complex. The layering can get as intricate as you like, but remember, the secret is—*be musical*.

● How's That Again?

Some composers have constructed whole pieces from the simplest of ideas—ideas that repeat over and over with changes of key, **orchestration** (instruments used), or **dynamic level** (loud and soft). The Norwegian composer Edvard Grieg (GREEG) wrote a piece for orchestra called *In the Hall of the Mountain King*. The basic rhythm of the theme is

and the basic melodic idea is

As you listen, you will hear almost no change in the rhythm, and the melody is constantly repeated. Which elements in the music <u>do</u> change?

Peer Gynt, "In the Hall of the Mountain King" ..... Grieg

Edvard Grieg
(1843–1907)

Meet the Composer

Grieg is so closely associated with the land and legends of Norway that few people realize his ancestry was Scottish. His grandfather (who spelled the name "Gr*eig*") had emigrated to Norway from Scotland around 1765.

Grieg was a *nationalist* composer, a composer whose national background was constantly reflected in his compositions. Nationalism, which was an important movement during the Romantic period, depended a great deal on folk music, as well as on music written to *sound* like folk music. Grieg chose to write his music so that it would capture the flavor of Norwegian folk music. His lyric melodies caused many people to call him the Chopin of the North.

3 + 2 + 2 = 7

On page 116 you began a study of meters. You learned about beats grouped in units, about those units being in groups of two, three, and four. And you even found that meter in 2 and meter in 3 could be combined in unusual ways, as in "Tumbalalaika," on page 120. Go back and look at the last section of "Tumbalalaika" where the meter is shown as $\frac{3}{4}$ $\frac{2}{4}$. Now imagine that the bar line between each $\frac{3}{4}$ measure and $\frac{2}{4}$ measure has been removed. How would you now express that larger measure in a meter signature? If you said, "Call it $\frac{5}{4}$," you were right. $\frac{5}{4}$ would be an accurate description of the meter of that last section—five beats per measure, with the quarter note (♩) representing the beat. Now listen to this "rap" piece. What do you think its meter is?

DANCIN'   *Sole to Soul*   Words by Connie Rybak

1	2	3	**1**	2	**1**	2
GIRLS					*BOYS*	
On	the	street,	Let's	dance,	Let's	dance,
Feel	the	beat,	Great	chance,	Great	chance,
Twist	and	roll	Clock	- wise,	Clock	- wise,
Keep	con	- trol	Rock	- wise,	Rock	- wise.
BOYS					*GIRLS*	
Try	the	stage,	Up,	down,	Up,	down,
It's	the	rage	Down	- town,	Down	- town,
Now	that	glide,	Toe	- heel,	Toe	- heel,
What	a	ride,	Un	- real,	Un	- real.
GIRLS					*BOYS*	
When	I	move	Free	- ly,	Free	- ly,
Trou -	bles	soothed,	See	me,	See	me,
Feel	my	best	Danc	- in',	Danc	- in',
Need	no	rest	Pranc -	in',	Pranc -	in'.
BOYS					*GIRLS*	
Add	more	voice,	Hear	ye,	Hear	ye,
It's	your	choice,	Clear	- ly,	Clear	- ly,
Danc -	in's	role,	Real	- ly,	Real	- ly,
EVERYONE						
Sole	to	soul.	*(stamp,*	*clap*	*stamp,*	*clap)*

© 1988 Connie Rybak

Did you guess that the meter is in 7? The text of *Dancin'* groups its beats into a pattern of **1** 2 3, **1** 2, **1** 2. Why, do you think, are the beats divided this way and not **1** 2, **1** 2, **1** 2 3 or **1** 2, **1** 2 3, **1** 2? (*Hint:* Look at the way the word accents fall.)

● Sing It in 7

Have you ever sung the song, "Oh, Susanna"? If you have you may remember that it is in duple meter—beats grouped in twos. Try singing this contemporary arrangement of Foster's tune. You can see from the meter signature that the meter is in 7. Look at the music. Can you tell just by looking at it which of the following beat groupings best fits the music?

1 2, 1 2 3, 1 2

1 2 3, 1 2, 1 2

1 2, 1 2, 1 2 3

Oh, Susanna

Words and Music by Stephen Foster   Arranged by Sol Berkowitz

Guitar: capo 3

I ___ came from Al - a - bam - a with my ban - jo on my
rained all night the day I left the weath - er it was

knee, I'm _ go - in' to Lou' - si - an - a my ___ true love for to see. It ___
dry, The _ sun _ so hot I froze to death, Su - san - na don't you

cry. ___ Oh, Su - san - na, ___ Oh, don't you cry for me, For I've

come from Al - a - bam - a with my ban - jo on my knee, For I've come from Al - a -

bam - a with a ban - jo on my knee. ___

● More Beats Again—Meter in 10

Can you count the meter of this piece by Leonard Bernstein? Believe it or not, it's in a meter of 10! Bernstein, a well-known American composer and former conductor of the New York Philharmonic, suggests that the meter in 10 be broken down this way: 1 2, 1 2 3, 1 2, 1 2 3—really a kind of counting in two groups of five!

The section from which this excerpt is taken is based on the original Hebrew text of Psalm 131. The excerpt begins in the middle of the measure with the words *Adonai, Adonai.* The beat will be

| 6 | 7 | 8 | 9 | 10 | 1 | 2 | 3 | 4 | 5 | 6 | 7 | 8 | 9 | 10 | 1 | 2 | 3 | 4 | 5 |

*A - do - nai, A - do - nai,*_____   *Lo ga - vah__   li - bi,*_____

Now it's up to you. Can you follow the line above and then continue to count the beats in the rest of the piece? Don't worry if you get lost. One of Bernstein's reasons for using this unusual meter may have been to obscure the beat grouping so that the listener *wouldn't* know what meter it was in. He may have wanted a feeling of no clear beat grouping at all!

Leonard Bernstein and Queen Elizabeth II of England

Chichester Psalms (excerpt) . . . . Bernstein

BEATS WITHIN BEATS (OR 6, 3, OR 2?)

Why is a football field divided into five-yard lengths? Why not one-yard lengths or even one-*foot* lengths? Can you imagine what that football field would look like with one-foot divisions? Probably like a picket fence! Obviously, such small divisions would confuse the eye of the football fan sitting high up in the bleachers.

Sometimes the tempo of a piece of music is so fast that individual beats, like individual feet and yards, go by too quickly to be counted comfortably and without confusion. If you play any piece at all you can probably play "Chopsticks." Here it is in two different settings. One is slow, the other faster. Can you see any difference in the meter?

Try conducting each version. (You learned how to conduct meter in 3 on page 118.) Of course, now you're faced with a meter in 6, and you haven't learned how to conduct in 6 yet. Instead, try conducting in 2 (see page 116), three eighth notes to a beat, and see how it works. You see, like the football field that gathers up smaller units and lays them out in larger, easier-to-handle bunches, $\frac{6}{8}$ meter in a fast tempo turns a group of six beats into two large beats. To compound this situation further, it's almost as if you were conducting in 2, with every beat having a triplet! And to compound it even more, this kind of "meter-in-a-meter" is called *compound meter*.

Three as One

This song has a meter signature of $\frac{3}{8}$. Do you remember what that means? It means that there are three beats in each measure, and the eighth note (♪) represents one beat. But listen to the song once before you decide what the meter really is. How does it feel when you *sing* it?

Con el vito

Folk Song from Spain   English Version by Aura Kontra   Arranged by Darrel Peter

Con el vi - to, vi - to, vi - to, _____ Con el
kohn ehl vee - toh vee - toh vee - toh kohn ehl

vi - to, vi - to, va. _____ Con el vi - to, vi - to,
vee - toh vee - toh vah kohn ehl vee - toh vee - toh

vi - to, _____ Con el vi - to, vi - to, va. _____ To the
vee - toh kohn ehl vee - toh vee - toh vah U - na
oo - nah

bull - fights in Se - vi - lla, Went the Span - ish la - dy
ma - la - gue - ña fue a Se - vi - lla a ver los
mah - lah - ghen - nyah fweh ah seh - vee - yah ah vehr lohs

rid - ing; She was cap - tured on the high - way
to - ros; Y en la mi - tad del ca - mi - no
toh - rohs yehn lah mee - tahd dehl cah - mee - noh

By some Moor - ish ban - dits hid - ing.
La cau - ti - va - ron los mo - ros.
lah kow - tee - vah - rohn lohs moh - rohs

It goes like the wind, doesn't it? It would be impossible to conduct "Con el vito" in three. But if you understand that the beat is actually *one beat per measure* rather than three per measure as the signature would show, then it is easy. Try conducting just downbeats—one per measure—1 | 1 | 1 | 1 | 1 | 1 | and so on. You'll find that it works well. In some ways, just as $\frac{6}{8}$ can be rethought as $\frac{2}{\cdot}$, so the $\frac{3}{8}$ of "Con el vito" can be rethought as $\frac{1}{\cdot}$.

● Another Subdivision on the Musical Landscape

On the chart on page 123, you discovered that notes could be divided evenly into other notes, a quarter (♩) into two eighths (♫) or a half (♩) into two quarters (♩ ♩), for example. Composers, especially those who have been influenced by African rhythms, sometimes play little "accent games" with these subdivisions. Look at these quarter notes and their subdivided eighth notes.

Can you tell what has happened to the bottom line of eighth notes? Instead of the accents falling on the first of each two eighths (♫ ♫ ♫) as in the middle line, the accents are falling on the first of each *three* eighths (♫ ♫ ♫). It's almost as if a $\frac{6}{8}$ meter is being thrown against a $\frac{3}{4}$ meter. Listen to a group of percussionists playing the above pattern of **cross-rhythms,** then try it yourself.

Cross-rhythms

Now try playing the cross-rhythms yourself with the Zulu folk song *Mangwani Mpulele.*

Mangwani Mpulele . . . . Zulu Folk Song

AN "UNSQUARE" DANCE

While you may like the outfits in the left or middle pictures, many people might feel that the picture on the right shows a man who has dressed with taste. In the left picture he is wearing far too many colors. In the middle picture he is monochromatic—too much of one color. At the right he seems nicely coordinated.

Music also must have balance. There must be similar elements with a number of contrasting elements as well. Look at these melodies. Which has too much repetition? Too little repetition? Which is just right?

Dave Brubeck was looking for a way to both unify and give variety to this piece. As you listen, you may learn that it is in a meter of 7. (That's why it's called "unsquare.") Does the metric feeling have anything to do with its unity or variety?

Unsquare Dance .... Brubeck

Here is the meter scheme for *Unsquare Dance*. Try playing it on percussion instruments.

Meter	1	2	3	4	5	6	7
High instrument	x		x		x	x	
Low instrument	x		x		x		

You probably realized that it is the metric feel—acting as an ostinato throughout the piece—that acts as a unifier. The variations that Brubeck weaves over the ostinato provide variety and interest to this piece that is considered by many to be a twentieth-century jazz classic.

Dave Brubeck

DIAGRAMMING METER

	Unsquare Dance

The letters in the diagram for *Unsquare Dance* are the notes the string bass plays. The *x*'s are the hand claps heard throughout the piece. For "Rock Around the Clock," the diagram shows a pattern of chords that repeats throughout the song, beginning with the first verse. These bass notes, hand claps, and chord patterns help to give the pieces a unity—a "glue" that holds them together.

Set your bells up to play the triads with "Rock Around the Clock."

Rock Around the Clock

Words and Music by M. Freedman and J. Deknight

One, two, three-o'clock, four o'clock rock! Five, six, sev-en o'clock, eight o' clock rock!

Nine, ten, e-lev-en o'clock, Twelve o' clock rock. We're gon-na rock a-round the

clock to-night! 1. Put your glad rags on join me, hon,'__ we'll have some fun when the
chimes ring five six and sev-en, ⁊ we'll be right in____

clock strikes one, We're gon-na rock a-round the clock to-night, — we're gon-na
sev-enth heav'n, We're gon-na rock a-round the clock to-night, — we're gon-na

rock, rock, rock 'til the broad day-light, — We're gon-na rock, we're gon-na rock a-round —
rock, rock, rock 'til the broad day-light, — We're gon-na rock, we're gon-na rock a-round —

— the clock — to night. ————————— 2. When the clock strikes two,
— the clock — to night. ————————— 4. When it's eight, nine, ten, e -

three and four, if the band slows down we'll yell for more, We're gon-na rock a-round the
lev-en, too, I'll be go-in' strong and so will you, We're gon-na rock a-round the

clock to-night, — we're gon-na rock, rock, rock 'til the broad day-light, — We're gon-na
clock to-night, — we're gon-na rock, rock, rock 'til the broad day-light, — We're gon-na

rock, we're gon-na rock — a-round ——— the clock — to-night. ——   3. When the
rock, we're gon-na rock — a-round ——— the clock — to-night. ——

5. When the clock strikes twelve, we'll cool off. Then — start-a

rock - in' 'round the clock a - gain, — We're gon-na rock a-round the

clock to-night, — we're gon-na rock, rock, rock, 'til the broad day-light, — We're gon-na

rock, we're gon-na rock — a-round ——— the clock — to-night. ——

BLUESIN' ON THE BOTTOM, ROCKIN' ON THE TOP

Joe Turner Blues . . . . Traditional

You have heard a 12-bar blues. Both *Unsquare Dance* (in its divided-measure version) and "Rock Around the Clock" are loosely based on a chord progression used in the 12-bar blues. That is a three-phrase pattern of twelve measures with the chord progression:

I   I   I   I₇   IV₇   IV₇   I   I   V₇   IV₇   I   I

"It's Not So Easy Bein' Me" is based on the blues pattern in E♭ major. To build a harmonic accompaniment in the key of E♭, you will need I, IV, and V chords in that key. To make the chords even "bluesier," add a *seventh* on top of the chords.

It's Not So Easy Bein' Me

Words and Music by Lawrence Eisman

1. I don't see — why there must be — so man-y do's and don'ts in our so-
   know that I — am not the best — at an-y-thing I do, I fall be-
3. I don't see — why I must be — so caught up in a race for pop-u-

ci-e-ty, — Which seem de-signed — with me in mind — as
hind the rest, — It's not that I — don't care or try, — it's
lar-i-ty, — To live my life — through oth-er's eyes — when

if I did-n't know how to act re-fined. — If you'd look — I'm
e-ven got me fooled 'cause I won-der why, — It would help — if
I'm the on-ly one I must sat-is-fy, — I'd feel re-lieved — if

sure you'd see — It's not so eas-y be-in' me. — 2. I
you would see — It's not so eas-y be-in' me. —
you'd be-lieve, — It's not so eas-y be-in' me. —

A Rock Progression We Have Known and Loved—I VI IV V₇

If you can play "Chopsticks" on the piano, you can probably play
"Heart and Soul" as well. (It's usually done as a duet with a friend.)
The chord progression is I VI IV V₇ in the key of C. Play these
chords on bells or piano to go with "Those Magic Changes."

C   A min   F   G₇
I   VI   IV   V₇

Those Magic Changes

from *Grease*

Guitar: capo 5

Words and Music by Warren Casey and Jim Jacobs

C   C   C___   C   C,   A   A   A___   A mi-nor,   F   F   F___   F   F   F,

1.,2. G₇ D₇
G   G   G___   G   sev-en.

3. G₇ D₇
G   sev-en.

Solo C G
What's that play-ing on the
I'll   be   wait-ing by the

Am Em
ra-di-o,___   Why   do   I___   start sway-ing   to   and fro?___
ra-di-o,___   You'll come back_   to   me some   day,   I   know;_

C G
I   have nev-   er   heard that   song be-fore,_   But   if   I___   don't hear it
Been so   lone-some since your   last good-bye,_   But,   I'm   sing-ing as   I

G₇ D₇
an-y-more,_   It's   still   fa-mil-iar   to   me, Sends a   thrill_   right through me,
cry-ay-ay,__   While the bass_   is sound-ing, While the drums_   are   pound-ing,

F C
'Cause those chords re-mind me   of   the   night that   I   first fell   in   love to
Beat-ing   of   my   bro-ken heart will   climb to   first place   on   the   chart,_

THE FIREBIRD—A FLIGHT OF PATTERNS

Igor Stravinsky's colorful ballet tells the story of an old Russian folk tale. Prince Ivan, lost in a forest, finds a marvelous bird with flaming red feathers. He captures her but then, seeing that she is frightened, releases her. In gratitude the firebird gives the prince one of her feathers to protect him against evil, and she pledges her help should he ever be in trouble. Ivan meets a princess who with her twelve sisters is held prisoner by the evil King Katschei, (KAHT shay). Katschei tries to cast a spell on Ivan, but Ivan overcomes the wicked sorcerer with his firebird feather. The firebird appears and, placing Katschei in a trance, tells Ivan that Katschei's power lies in a monstrous egg, which she reveals to Ivan. The egg is broken, Katschei perishes, the princess and all of Katschei's prisoners are freed. Ivan and his princess are married in a sumptuous finale. The finale begins with a simple melodic phrase played slowly and quietly.

The melody becomes grander, nobler, almost like a fanfare.

Listen to the way Stravinsky builds textures and uses tone colors to create a satisfying ending to his ballet.

The Firebird, "Finale"........................Stravinsky

A scene from "The Firebird"

CAREERS IN MUSIC—COMPOSING

Although still a young composer, Suzanne Ciani (CHAH nee) has been composing for a good many years and has written a substantial body of work. Listen to Ciani as she discusses her life and work. Then listen to her *Composition for Synthesizer*. How does the composer alter the melody pattern? Do you hear a form?

Careers in Music—Suzanne Ciani
Composition for Synthesizer . . . . Ciani

IN UNITY THERE IS STRENGTH

Clap this rhythm.

Do you recognize that rhythm? If you said it's the rhythm of
"Twinkle, Twinkle, Little Star," you were right. And the rhythm
repeats and repeats exactly the same way for the entire song!

The repetition of the same two-measure rhythm pattern has a lot to
do with making the song feel unified—a feeling that it's all one
piece.

Try singing this patriotic song. Does your understanding of
"Twinkle, Twinkle, Little Star" give you a clue to a unifying element
in "America, the Beautiful"?

America, the Beautiful

Guitar: capo 3

Words by Katherine Lee Bates   Music by Samuel A. Ward   Countermelody by James W. Rooker mer - i - ca! _____ God shed His grace on thee, _____ And

mer - i - ca! A - mer - i - ca! God shed His grace on thee, And

mer - i - ca! A - mer - i - ca! God mend thine ev - 'ry flaw, Con -

crown thy good, From sea to shin - ing sea!

crown thy good with broth - er - hood, From sea to shin - ing sea!

firm thy soul in self - con - trol, Thy lib - er - ty in law!

3. O beautiful for heroes proved
   In liberating strife,
   Who more than self their country loved,
   And mercy more than life!
   America! America! May God thy gold refine,
   Till all success be nobleness,
   And ev'ry gain divine!

4. O beautiful for patriot dream
   That sees, beyond the years,
   Thine alabaster cities gleam
   Undimmed by human tears!
   America! America! God shed His grace on thee,
   And crown thy good with brotherhood,
   From sea to shining sea!

Even paintings can be based on one basic idea. What about this one? Can you see the single element that unifies the entire canvas?

THREE FLAGS   *Jasper Johns*

MANIPULATING A MOTIVE

Do you remember what a *motive* is? A motive is a very short musical fragment—usually only a few notes long—that a composer uses to build a piece. Do you remember building "In the Army," on page 44, from those little parts that preceded it? You were building from phrases there. A motive is even smaller. Look at this one.

Follow the score to see how Sol Berkowitz develops this six-note motive into a full composition for a keyboard instrument.

© 1985 Sol Berkowitz

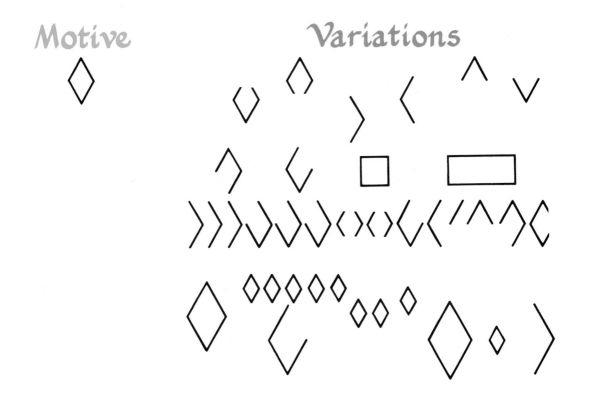

Motive   Variations

FROM PATTERN TO PIECE

On pages 168 and 169 you saw what Berkowitz can do with a
motive. Now let's go way back in time, to Johann Sebastian Bach, a
composer of the Baroque period who certainly made motive-building
look easy. Look at this motive.

How do you think Bach might have helped his motive grow? Here's
the first thing he did:

Listen for other ways Bach varied and expanded his motive.

Minuet..Bach

"On My Journey" starts with a distinctive melody and rhythm
pattern. How does the rest of the song grow from that pattern?

On My Journey

Relaxed African-American Traditional Song Arranged by Lawrence Eisman
New Verses by Erik Darling, Lee Hays, Fred Hellerman and Ronnie Gilbert

1. When I'm on my jour-ney,__ don't you weep af-ter me,__
2. Ev-'ry lone-ly riv-er__ must go home to the sea,__

When I'm on my jour-ney,__ don't you weep af-ter me,__
Ev-'ry lone-ly riv-er__ must go home to the sea,__

When I'm on my jour-ney,__ don't you weep af-ter me,__ I don't
Ev-'ry lone-ly riv-er__ must go home to the sea,__

want you to weep af-ter me.____

Discern Those Devices! (That Means Recognize Them)

So far we have talked about repetition and inversion (in "Manipulations"), among other compositional devices that composers use. Do you remember discussing sequences on page 111? You will find repetition, inversion, and sequence in each of these songs. In "If I Were You," many measures are empty. How would you fill them, based on the motive in the first two measures?

If I Were You

Words by Connie Rybak Music by Lawrence Eisman

1. If you were me and I were you, no one would know who was who.
2. If you were me and I were you, we'd bet-ter plan what we'd do.

We'd look the same, just change our views, ex - ter - nal - ly, give no clues.
I'd be the brains, you'd have the looks, Har-vard's my choice; You? No books.

Our fam - i - lies might get con - fused if it were you in my shoes.
Since you're so shy, and I am not, think of the deeds we could plot.

What a great trick, Oh, what a switch, spirits re - versed, which is which?
I'd take your place, get you a date, just like a worm, serve as bait.

© 1985 Connie Rybak

By the Waters of Babylon

Words from the Psalms   Music by Philip Hayes (Adapted)

I
By _____ the wa - ters, the wa - ters of Bab - y - lon,

II
We lay down and wept, __ and wept, __ for Zi - on, When

III
we re-mem - ber thee, re-mem - ber thee, re-mem - ber Zi - on.

FILLING OUT FORMS

The Brandenburg Gate (Berlin, East Germany)

"That building has an interesting form." "The form of that automobile makes it look like a sports car." "I don't understand this painting. It doesn't seem to have a logical form."

Everything has **form.** Cars. Trains. Bikes. Even you. We recognize things by their form. Form is a combination of things that are alike and things that are different. In music, form is created by putting like and unlike sections together. "In the Army," on page 44, had two contrasting sections, one labeled *A*, the other labeled *B*. Do you remember what you did at the end of section B? The *D.S. al Fine* (FEE nay) told you to go back to the beginning of section A and sing to the *Fine* (an Italian word that means "end"). When you did that you had a form that could be labeled *ABA*.

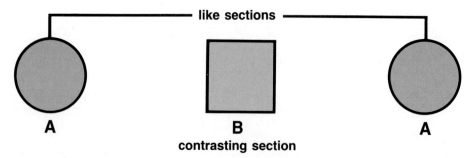

The ABA form became so common to song writers that it has become known as song form. Think of the popular songs you know; you may find that many of them are in ABA form!

Why is the structure shown on page 172, the Brandenburg Gate in Berlin, labeled ABA? Do you see that it has three sections? Do you see that the two end sections (the buildings) are alike and that the middle section (the columned gate) is different?

What is the form of "A Mighty Fortress Is Our God," on page 276? What is the form of "By the Waters of Babylon," on page 171? And how about "You're Never Fully Dressed Without a Smile," on page 109? Its form is . . . ?

Now listen to this well-known march. Can you figure out its form? Careful, it's complicated.

Washington Post March . . . . .Sousa

Can you identify the form of this song? The sections have been labeled to help you recognize them.

Courtesy of the United States Marine Corps

Rondo—Music's Boomerang

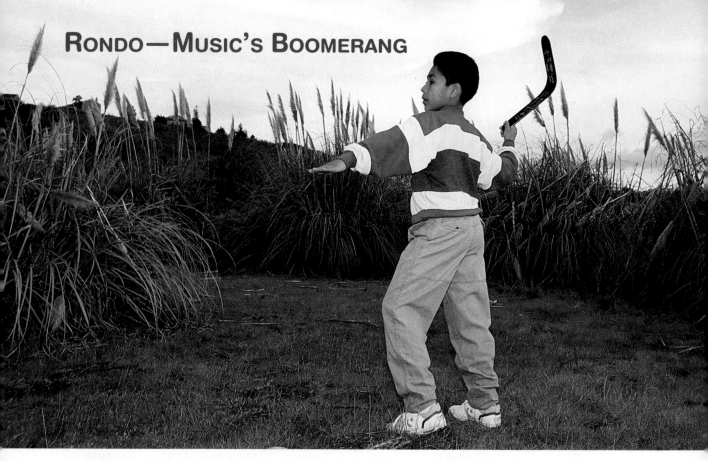

Just like a boomerang properly thrown, a rondo theme always comes back again. Listen to this famous march. Can you hear anything recurring?

 Colonel Bogey March . . . . Alford

After a short introduction you should have heard section A, section B, a return of A, then a totally *new* section, section C. Listen again and follow the chart to hear what happens next. Notice that there are two letters in most of the sections. That's because the melody sometimes repeats before going on to the next section.

Introduction   Interlude

● A Rondo by Beethoven

If you have studied piano for more than a few years, you may have played this well-known piano piece. As you listen to it, follow the Call Chart to hear the **rondo** form.

Für Elise .... Beethoven

1	**2**	**3**	**4**	**5**
(A)	[B]	(A)	(C)	(A)

Now, here's a rondo to sing. Try "Dodi Li."

Dodi Li

Guitar: capo 5

Words Traditional   Music by Nira Chen   English Words by Dav ben Shmuel

Chorus

There a - wait - ing, cap - ti - vat - ing,
Wake the North Wind, wake the South Wind,
Li - bav - ti - ni a - cho - ti ka - la
lee - bahv - tee - nee ah - khoh - tee kah - lah

My dear and love - ly bride.
And send her to my side.
li - bav - ti - ni ka - la.
lee - bahv - tee - nee kah - lah

Solo

For my love
Do - di li
doh - dee lee

is a shep - herd tend - ing flocks a - mong the fields.
va - 'a - ni lo ha - ro - e ba - sho - sha - nim.
vah - ah - nee loh hah - roh - ay bah-shoh-shah-neem

Chorus

For my love is a shep - herd tend - ing flocks
Do - di li va - 'a - ni lo ha - ro - e
doh - dee lee vah - ah - nee loh hah - roh - ay

a tempo

a - mong the fields.
ba - sho - sha - nim.
bah - shoh - shah - neem.

Minuet .... Bach

Listen to this minuet and follow the music. You will see that there are boxes around some of the notes. By looking and listening you should be able to tell if the intervals are *steps, leaps,* or *repeats.* Write your answer in the box by putting S for step, L for leap, and R for repeat.

Minuet

by J. S. Bach

TEST 6

Write the letter of the correct answer in the blank.

1. Melodies move by _____ , _____ , and _____ .
   a. step
   b. reverse
   c. leap
   d. repeat

2. A major scale is a pattern of whole steps and _____ .
   a. half backs
   b. half beats
   c. whole notes
   d. half steps

3. A key signature shows what _____ are needed.
   a. sharps or naturals
   b. sharps or flats
   c. heels or flats
   d. flats or naturals

4. A minor scale sounds different from a major scale because it has a different _____ .
   a. step pattern
   b. melody
   c. key signature
   d. rhythm

5. A scale of only five notes, with a step-and-a-half between the third and fourth notes is called _____ .
   a. a pentatonic scale
   b. a twelve-tone scale
   c. a fish scale
   d. a chromatic scale

6. In a *sequence,* a melodic pattern is repeated _____ .
   a. at higher or lower levels
   b. once
   c. backwards
   d. with other instruments

7. In music, an interval is the span between two _____ .
   a. rests
   b. key signatures
   c. notes
   d. bar lines

8. "This Land Is Your Land" was written by _____ .
   a. Arlo Guthrie
   b. Tyrone Guthrie
   c. Woody Guthrie
   d. Frederick Guthrie

TEST 7

Circle T if the statement is true; circle F if the statement is false.

1. When every other beat is accented, it is called meter in 3.

    T   F

2. A meter signature shows how many notes are in each measure.

    T   F

3. In a meter of 4, the accent falls on the first of every four beats.

    T   F

4. When different meters follow each other in a composition, it is called *multimeter*.

    T   F

5. In notation, the largest note unit is the sixteenth note.

    T   F

TEST 8

Circle T if the statement is true; circle F if the statement is false.

1. When three notes are squeezed into the space of two, they are called trios.

T   F

2. A well-known American composer who wrote many rags at the beginning of the twentieth century was William Billings.

T   F

3. The word *accelerando* means "getting faster."

T   F

4. Harmony is the sounding of two or more tones together.

T   F

5. The way a voice or instrument sounds is called its *tone color*.

T   F

TEST 9

Circle the correct answer.

1. A pattern that repeats over and over.

music   ostinato

2. In *In the Hall of the Mountain King,* Grieg repeats this over and over.

the melody   the orchestration

3. A Romantic-period style saw the use of it.

folk music   harpsichord music

4. Some metric patterns are in 5, 7, even 10! In your book, Sol Berkowitz wrote an arrangement of Stephen Foster's "Oh, Susanna." What meter was it in?

3   5   7   10

5. Some meters, like $\frac{6}{8}$ or $\frac{12}{8}$, are often thought of as being "inside" other meters. What are these meters called?

complex meters   simple meters   compound meters

6. Music is usually given shape by repetition and contrast of sections. What is this called?

harmony   ostinato   riffs   form

7. An often-used form that is diagramed as ABACA has this name.

song form   rondo   sonata-allegro   ABA

MAKING MUSIC

PERFORMING IN ENSEMBLES

The conductor enters to resounding applause. The orchestra is asked to rise and share the accolade with him or her. The audience will not applaud again until after the piece is finished, not even after individual movements within the piece. The contrast between the silence during the performance and the clamor at the end is drama in itself.

Do you remember singing "Ode to Joy," on page 135? Try singing it again, and then listen to the way it is used in this selection, the finale to Beethoven's *Ninth Symphony*.

   Symphony No. 9 in D Minor, Movement 4 (excerpt)......
....Beethoven

That was quite a performance! In contrast, there is the soloist making music all alone. Listen to Jill Trinka, a teacher and folk singer, sing an old folk song, *Johnny Has Gone for a Soldier,* accompanying herself on the mountain dulcimer.

   Johnny Has Gone for a Soldier ..... American Folk Song

Building an Ensemble

Here is a line from a song that could be sung by a soloist.

Let's add another part. Of course, now it is no longer a **solo,** it's a **duet.**

Add another part and the song becomes a **trio**—an ensemble of three performers, like the song, "Laredo," on page 186.

Try singing "Laredo." Usually, when there are three parts, they are divided between two staffs to make them easier to read. In "Laredo," however, the three parts are all on one staff so you can best see their relationship. If the three parts are hard to sing together at first, work them out one at a time. You can build them up just the way a bricklayer lays bricks—one layer at a time.

Laredo

Mexican Folk Song   English Words by Margaret Marks

1. I'm off for La - re - do, fare-well my love, I'm sor - ry to cause you
2. I've brought you a hand-sewn sad - dle, my love, A blan - ket and bri - dle

pain; I prom-ise to send a let - ter, my love, To say when we'll meet a -
fine; So when you go past the bunk-house, my love, The cow-boys will know you're

gain. Don't fol - low a - cross the prai - rie, my love, Don't
mine. I've brought you a key of sil - ver, my love, At -

fol - low me where I go, But wait till I send a
tached to a gold - en chain, To lock up your heart for -

mes - sage, my love, Till then I will miss you so.
ev - er, my love, If nev - er we meet a - gain.

A Popular Trio

A few years ago there was a very popular singing trio called the
Andrews Sisters. They were very well known for their movie
appearances and for their tireless efforts to entertain military units
overseas during World War II. Listen to this selection performed by
LaVerne, Maxene, and Patti Andrews. A big hit at one time, it still
shows off a special close-harmony sound like that of "Laredo."

Boogie-Woogie Bugle Boy . . . . **Prince/Raye**

The Andrews Sisters

● Close Harmony of a Different Kind

Men can sing in close harmony, too. (Close harmony, by the way, just means harmony in which the chord tones are close together, giving it a very rich, bright sound. It is this ♭̸═ instead of this ♭̸═ .)

During the 1950s and early 1960s, a male **quartet** called the Hi-Los sang, like the Andrews Sisters, in close harmony. Of course, since there were four of them, they could sing an extra note in each chord. And by this time, harmony was much thicker in texture and often included notes in the chords that were *dissonant,* not in harmony with the chord. Listen to this group sing a pop version of an old African-American spiritual.

Swing Low, Sweet Chariot ... African-American Spiritual

TWO PARTS—DUET AND CHORUS

Do you remember what a song for two vocal parts is called? If you said *duet,* you're right. Step up and win the prize at Coney Island! What's the prize? A chance to sing this familiar song about New York's well-known amusement park. If you sing it as a group (half the class on part 1, the other half on part 2), you've formed a **chorus**!

Coney Island Baby

Words and Music by Les Applegate

Your version of "Coney Island Baby" is arranged in two parts. If two more parts could be added, the song would be a quartet. "Coney Island Baby" is a staple of the barbershop quartet repertoire. When men or women sing in barbershop style, the melody is in the second voice from the top. The voice above the melody, the specific kinds of chord progressions, as well as the close harmony, all combine to give the barbershop quartet its special sound. Listen to this one.

Coney Island Baby . . . . *Applegate*

It's All in the Family

On page 140 you learned that instruments come in four basic families—woodwinds, brass, percussion, and strings. You can form your own percussion ensemble. The score below calls for two pitched percussion instruments (glockenspiel and resonator bells), and a line is provided for nonpitched instruments (finger cymbals, claves, tambourines). You can see that the player of the nonpitched percussion instruments must change instruments during the piece. You can add instruments as you like so that as many can play as possible.

Beating the Blahs

Mary E. Hoffman (Adapted)

THE PEOPLE'S CHOICE

Music, music, music. There doesn't seem to be any group of people anywhere on earth that hasn't developed a rich musical life. Whether among the Inuit (IH noo iht) in their frozen homeland far above the Arctic Circle or among the Jívaro (HEE vah roh) Indians deep in the steaming jungles of Brazil's Mato Grosso, music can be found. The groups sing, and they make instruments by hand from whatever materials are available. Listen to the drumming of a short piece by the Yorubas, a group you discussed on page 12.

Yoruba Dance . . . . Traditional African

Yoruba tribesmen playing donno drums

West Indian steel drum band

● An Unusual Instrument

In the West Indies of the early twentieth century, ships delivered oil
in large steel drums. The island residents found many uses for the
empty drums, including one use that has come to symbolize the
West Indies—as instruments for the steel drum band. People found
that hitting the steel drums in different ways produced different
pitches and that smaller drums had a higher sound than larger ones
did. The residents found that by denting the tops of the drums, they
could produce a scale. Finally they realized that cutting the drum in
half increased its resonance. Listen to a steel drum band.

El Merecumbe . . . . Steel Drum Band

● Sin ellos no hay fiesta!
(Without Them There's No Party!)

In Mexico a very special kind of ensemble developed. The musicians are called *mariachis* (mah ree AH chees) and their ensemble is called a mariachi band. The music they make takes on a special sound quite unlike anything else you may have heard. The **instrumentation** usually consists of violins, guitars, and trumpets. And, of course, the mariachis sing as well! You can find these groups wherever there is a celebration—a *fiesta*—playing their infectious folk and popular melodies and rhythms. Listen to this mariachi band perform *Cielito lindo*.

Cielito lindo . . . . Traditional Mexican

Mexican mariachi band

The Sound of the Highlands

Think of Scotland and what do you think of? Kilts? Heather? Haunted castles on the heath? You might think of these things, and then you might think of the bagpipe. Of course, many European countries have bagpipes—including Ireland, Spain, and Czechoslovakia—but somehow the Scottish folk seem to have made it most their own.

Scottish bagpipe player

The bagpipe is an ancient folk instrument. Mention was even made of it in imperial Rome! Although the bagpipe looks complicated, it is really rather simple. The large bag is a bellows that blows air through the pipes. The player holds the bag under his or her arm and squeezes to get the air moving. The long pipe in the player's mouth is *not* what makes the sound. The player blows into the pipe to keep a steady supply of air in the bag. The sounding pipe is the small one fingered by the player. And the large pipes? You might think that they provide harmony, and they do, in a way. But they only play *one* pitch each—they are drones. It is this combination of drone and melody that gives the bagpipe that unique sound that many call "the sound of the Highlands."

Listen to this bagpipe player.

Bagpipe Music—"Barren Rocks of Aden" and "Scotland, the Brave" .... Traditional Scottish

Jazz Ensembles

You have probably sung or heard this song before. Sing it now.

When the Saints Go Marching In

African-American Spiritual

Guitar: capo 3

1. Oh, when the saints go march-ing in,

1. Oh, when the saints go march-ing in,

Oh, when the saints go march - ing in,

Oh, when the saints go march - ing in,

Oh, Lord, I want to be in that num - ber,

Oh, Lord, I want to be in that num - ber,

When the saints go march - ing in.

When the saints go march - ing in.

2. Oh, when the stars refuse to shine, . . .

3. Oh, when I hear that trumpet sound, . . .

The people of New Orleans developed a very special kind of ensemble—the Dixieland band. In Dixieland jazz, the melody is played by everyone, and then each player in turn improvises on the melody while all the others provide a little harmonic support. It is polite to applaud after each solo. Dixieland bands are not usually very large—five or six people at the most. Again, this style of ensemble playing has its own unique sound. Listen to what this group does with "When the Saints Go Marching In."

When the Saints Go Marching In . . . .
. . . .**African-American Spiritual**

The Dixieland band was one of the first jazz ensembles, and the jazz ensemble is still a very important part of the music scene. Listen to the Modern Jazz Quartet play a piece describing the Golden Striker, a figure on a clock tower in Venice, Italy. The instruments are piano, vibraphone, string bass, and percussion. Listen for the finger cymbals played at various times.

The Golden Striker, **"No Sun in Venice"** . . . . .Lewis

The Golden Striker (Venice, Italy)

A Classic Jazz Ensemble

Among the jazz musicians of the last few years, a certain few names ring like no others—Charlie "Bird" Parker, Stan Kenton, Miles Davis, Pete Fountain, Al Hirt, Dave Brubeck, Dizzy Gillespie, Chick Corea. Dave Brubeck and his quartet were one of the most popular jazz ensembles for a long time. His experiments with rhythm and meter (Remember *Unsquare Dance* on page 157?) took him out of conventional jazz playing and made him one of the most influential jazz musicians.

Listen to the Dave Brubeck Quartet play *Camptown Races*. The instruments are piano, saxophone, bass, and percussion. You will hear that both the piano and the saxophone get a chance to improvise on the melody. Improvisation? You've heard that word before. That's what jazz is all about. You've heard it in each jazz piece you've listened to.

Camptown Races .... Foster/Brubeck

THE VOCAL BACKUPS

You've heard them. The singer appears live on a talk show or a recent rock video and sings his or her latest hit (or flop). Suddenly, from nowhere, you hear voices with the singer. Do they come from the beyond? More likely from the recording studio. These are backup singers. They are heard on the accompaniment tape (the "track" tape) that the singer uses when appearing on television. (Of course, backup singers may also perform "live" on stage with the soloist.) They're part of the arrangement. Sometimes they may sing words. At other times they may sing neutral syllables, such as *ah* or *oo*.

You can add vocal parts behind an existing composition. Listen to this piece by Philip Glass. You will notice that the music seems to change very little. There are only a few ideas repeated again and again. Repetition is an important device for building a composition in this style, called *minimalism* (so called because the minimalist composer tries to create works using the minimal of materials). This music is a little like watching a lake in which the same small wave motions repeat over and over, changing only slightly.

LISTENING LIBRARY *The Photographer,* "A Gentleman's Honor" . . . . Glass

You could probably hear slight variations as the piece went on. The one unchanging element was the eight-measure chord pattern:

A min. | A min. | F maj. | F maj. | G | G$_7$ | A min. | A min. |

You can do a vocal backup to the piece by singing the progression.

Of course you will need some words and rhythm to make it effective. Try

do   wah_____   do wah_____   do wah_ do wah_ do wah_____

Or you might try

doot 'n' do wah_   doot 'n' do wah_ | and so forth.

Think up some rhythm patterns of your own. There are many that will fit.

FOLLOWING A SCORE

"There are so many things going on! How can it all be kept together?"

Looking to the right at a reduced page from an instrumental score, you may very well wonder how composers and conductors deal with all those different parts at once. On the next few pages, you'll get an idea of what it's like to follow several different types of scores. Let's start off with just the melody of a song.

Young Person's Guide to the Orchestra — Benjamin Britten. © Copyright 1946 by Hawkes and Son (London) Ltd.; Renewed 1973. Reprinted by permission of Boosey & Hawkes, Inc.

Glee Reigns in Galilee
(Gilu Hagalilim)

Hebrew Folk Song   English Words by Dav ben Shmuel

Guitar:

Em

Be joy - ful, Ga - li - le - ans, raise up your voic - es;
Gi - lu ha - ga - li - lim gi - bo - rei he - cha - yil;
ghee - loo hah - gah - lee - leem ghee - boh - rai heh - khah - yeel

Em

Be glad, be joy - ful___ morn - ing and eve - ning.
Si - su v' - sim - chu___ yo - mam va - la - yil.
see - soo vuh - seem - khoo yoh - mahm vah - lah - yeel

G

Be joy - ful, Ga - li - le - ans, raise up your voic - es;
Gi - lu ha - ga - li - lim gi - bo - rei he - cha - yil;
ghee - loo hah - gah - lee - leem ghee - boh - rai heh - khah - yeel

G

Be glad, be joy - ful___ morn - ing and eve - ning.
Si - su v' - sim - chu___ yo - mam va - la - yil.
see - soo vuh - seem - khoo yoh - mahm vah - lah - yeel

Here's the same song with piano accompaniment. Remember, the voice part is always on the top line, so it's easy to keep your place.

● The Full Score

A full score can be of many sizes, from the smallest trio or quartet
to the most instrument-packed or orchestral pieces. In a full score
each instrument of the ensemble is shown on its own staff. If there
are four instruments playing four different parts, there are four
staffs. If there are ninety instruments playing ninety different parts,
there are ninety staffs. Obviously, the last score is going to be of
considerable size!

Here is our song from page 200 scored for an instrumental ensemble
made up of flute, trumpet, trombone, percussion, and bass. Follow
the score as you listen to the recording. (As on the previous pages,
the melody is highlighted in yellow as it skips from instrument to
instrument.)

Glee Reigns in Galilee
(Gilu Hagalilim)

Hebrew Folk Song

PASS THE THEME, PLEASE!

Composers often like to pass a theme from one instrument or voice
to another. Being able to read a score is very important in helping
to keep track of these wandering themes. In this score the arrows
will help you keep track of where you are as the melody passes from
voice to voice. (Remember "Glee Reigns in Galilee" on page 202?)

Let It Snow

Words by Sammy Cahn   Music by Jule Styne   Arranged by Daniel Shigo

You Can't Tell the Players Without a Score

Look at the opening page of the full score for Benjamin Britten's
Young Person's Guide to the Orchestra.

This is what the score looks like when it shows all the instruments.
(The color tints were added here to help you see the different
instrument groups.) The woodwinds are at the top in green, the
brass are next in red, then come the percussion instruments in
yellow, and the strings are at the bottom in blue. Why, do you
suppose, are the strings at the bottom in an orchestral score?
Because when orchestras first began to organize, they were most
commonly strings-only orchestras. As other instruments were added,
they were placed on staffs above the strings.

Young Person's Guide to the Orchestra Benjamin Britten.

Young Person's Guide to the Orchestra—Benjamin Britten.
© Copyright 1946 by Hawkes and Son (London) Ltd;
Renewed 1973. Reprinted by permission of Boosey & Hawkes, Inc.

CALL CHART 9

Listen to a Call Chart and find the appropriate instrument group in the score. Remember those colors. It will help you find them.

Young Person's Guide to the Orchestra,
"Introduction" ....Britten

1 Full orchestra

2 Woodwinds

3 Brass

4 Strings

5 Percussion

6 Full orchestra

Benjamin Britten
(1913–1976)

Meet the Composer

Benjamin Britten has been hailed by some as Great Britain's greatest composer since Henry Purcell, a Baroque-period composer. His many vocal and instrumental pieces have charmed the listening public since he first gained acclaim as a young prodigy. Perhaps his best known works are his operas, of which *Peter Grimes* is considered his masterpiece. Several other stage works, including *A Midsummer Night's Dream* and the spooky *The Turn of the Screw,* are widely performed.

Britten's output has also included a great deal of instrumental as well as non-operatic vocal music. His chamber music works with voice, such as *Serenade for Tenor, Horn, and Strings,* are considered by many to be among the finest small ensemble writing in the twentieth century. And his large choral pieces, such as *A Ceremony of Carols* and *War Requiem,* have been hailed by critics as contemporary masterpieces.

CAREERS IN MUSIC—CONDUCTING

A conductor must be on the ball to keep track of all those instruments. Listen to what one prominent conductor, Eve Queler, has to say about conducting.

Careers in Music—Eve Queler

Le Cid, "Aragonaise" . . . . Massenet

DON'T GO ANYWHERE WITHOUT A SONG

● A Theme Musical by Carmino Ravosa

Want to put on a show? You can, you know. You'll find the makings of a show right here on the next few pages. The script will give you a beginning, an end, and a hook (a unifying idea that catches an audience's attention). Your show can be big or small. You can follow the script, using the songs suggested, or you can use other songs from the book or even from outside the book.

For staging you can use a few multilevel boxes, perhaps painted in vivid colors. Use your imagination. Just remember, you and the songs are the most important parts of the show!

● On with the Show

Stage is empty . . . "Don't Go Anywhere Without a Song" is played as a student makes his or her way on stage.)

STUDENT: Our show is all about songs. There's no scenery, and no costumes . . . just songs with a few words in between to tie them together.

There's magic in songs. Whether you're sad, happy, bored, down, blue, whether you feel like quitting or you're on top of the world, there's a song that's just right to express your feeling. So—don't go anywhere without a song!
(As the song is sung, performers appear from all over the auditorium and take their places on stage.)

Don't Go Anywhere Without a Song

Words and Music by Carmino Ravosa

© 1985 Carmino Ravosa

where with - out a song.

Don't get caught with - out ___ one.
If you're caught in traf - fic

Who knows what life will bring?
or if you're feel - ing ill.

Wher - ev - er you may
A song is sure to

be, _____
help, _____

Have a song to sing.
If there's an - y thing that will.

song.

Now go into any songs you'd like. Just write your own lead-in. For example: "Sometimes you get caught up in school, rushing around, working, trying to save time. Here's how one songwriter felt about time."

Song: "Time in a Bottle," page 300

STUDENT: When people get up in the morning, they put on their slacks or skirts, or perhaps their jeans, a shirt, socks, shoes—and now they're ready for the day, right?

Wrong! You're not fully dressed yet. Go back to the mirror.

Song: "You're Never Fully Dressed Without a Smile," page 109

STUDENT: Got a good friend? When was the last time you told him (her) how important he (she) was?

Song: "I'd Do Anything," page 230

STUDENT: Before you can like others or just one special person, you've got to like yourself first. And, you know, I've got some philosophy on that.

I Like Me

Words and Music by Carmino Ravosa

Solo 1st time, chorus 2nd time

If I can smile ___ and do some-thing worth-while, _ I like me.

If I can give ___ ev-'ry day that I live, ___ I like me.

If I can boast ___ that I've giv-en my most, ___ I like me. If

each day I plan ___ to give some-one a hand, ___ I like me. If I can

look at my-self ___ in the mir-ror each night ___ and I learn the dif -

- f'rence be-tween wrong and right, ___ Then I can say ___ at the

end of each day, I like me. me.

STUDENT: And when friendship really clicks, it's wonderful. There's nothing quite like a really good friend. When a friend is around, you can bet everything's coming up roses.

Everything's Coming Up Roses

from *Gypsy*

Words by Stephen Sondheim   Music by Jule Styne

Things look swell,   Things look great,   Gon - na
Clear the decks,   Clear the tracks,   We got

have the whole world___ on a plate.   Start - ing
noth - ing to do___ but re - lax.   Blow a

here,_____ Start - ing now,_____ hon - ey,
kiss,_____ Take a bow,_____ hon - ey,

Ev - 'ry - thing's com - ing___ up ros - es!
Ev - 'ry - thing's com - ing___ up ros - es!

Now's our___ in - ning.___ Stand the world on its ear!_

Set it___ spin - ning___ That - 'll be just the be -

gin - ning!___ Cur - tain up!   Light the lights!

We got noth - ing to hit___ but the heights!

We'll be swell,_____ We'll be great!_____ I can tell,_____

_— Just you wait!_____ _That luck - y star I talk a - bout is_

_due!_____ _Hon - ey, Ev - 'ry - thing's com - ing__ up_

_ros - es__ for me and__ for you._____

STUDENT: Sometimes it feels as if you have no friends at all. When
you feel like quitting something . . . I guess we all face that
sometimes . . . there must be a song for that kind of feeling.

Never Say Never

Words and Music by Carmino Ravosa

_Nev - er__ say nev - er,__ Nev - er__ say die. Yes, you _ can do it, __ that's if _ you try._

_Don't be _ a quit - ter_ and some day_ you'll win; Don't you _ give up and _ don't you _ give_

_in. Nev - er__ say nev - er,__ Nev - er__ say no, There is__ no doubt you_ can_

_do it, __ I know._____ Nev - er__ say nev - er._

OLIVER!

When *Oliver!* premiered in London in the early 1960s, and later on Broadway, it was an instant success. Many critics had felt that the stories of Charles Dickens were too highbrow for the popular theater. *Oliver!* proved them wrong. The score by Lionel Bart was attractive and inventive to many, and the show paved the way for other Dickens-inspired musicals on Broadway, in the movies, and on television. *Oliver!* proved that there is no subject that cannot be discussed on the Broadway stage.

Here is a kind of concert version of *Oliver!* that you and your classmates can perform. All you need is a narrator (if you use several, it is more interesting), a record player, and your own voice.

It will be effective to have some students mime the action. That is, act it out without words.

The Story of Oliver Twist

NARRATOR: In England the Poor Law of 1834 said that all able-bodied paupers must live in a workhouse. Families were separated. Hunger and abuse were common. In Britain during the early nineteenth century, poverty was considered a crime!

LISTENING LIBRARY   *Overture*

ACT I, SCENE 1
SETTING: A workhouse for paupers and orphans.
(*As music begins, children enter the room single file, moving toward assigned table locations. With all in place at tables, song begins.*)

Food, Glorious Food

Words and Music by Lionel Bart

What is ____ there more hand - some? ____ Gulped, swal - lowed, or chewed, ____
Don't care ____ what it looks like! ____ Burned, un - der - done, crude, ____

Still worth ____ a king's ran - som! ____ What is ____ it we
Don't care ____ what it cooks like! ____ Just think - ing of

dream a - bout, ____ what brings ____ on a sigh? _____ Piled peach-
grow - ing fat, ____ our sens - es go reel - ing ____ One mo -

1st Boy

- es and cream, a - bout six feet high! _____ Food, glo-
- ment of know - ing that full - up feel - ing! ____ Food, glo-

All

- ri - ous food, ____ eat right ____ through the men - u. ____
- ri - ous food, ____ what would - n't we give for ____

Mimic eating.

Just loos - en your belt ____ Two inch - es and then you ____
that ex - tra bit more? ____ That's all ____ that we live for. ____

Work up ____ a new ap - pe - tite ____ in this ____ in - ter -
Why should ____ we be fat - ed to ____ do no - thing but

2nd Boy   *All*   *3rd Boy*

lude, then, food, once ____ a - gain, food, fa - bu - lous
brood on food, no - thing but food, ma - gi - cal

food, glo - ri - ous food! _____

food, beau - ti - ful food, glo - ri - ous food! _____

(At the close of the song, Mr. Bumble walks onto the upper level; children turn their heads in his direction.)

NARRATOR 2: Mr. Bumble, the parish beadle, strides onto the upper level of the workhouse, accompanied by Widow Corney, the matron of the workhouse. He holds his mace in a taunting manner as all eyes turn toward him in fear. When the mace strikes the floor, the children file slowly to the vats of gruel, receive one ladle-ful, and return to their seats. Once seated, they remain motionless, awaiting the signal to begin eating. Bumble deliberately waits to strike the mace upon the floor, knowing that they are almost starved, and enjoying his position of authority.

NARRATOR 1: The meager rations are quickly devoured. All eyes now turn toward one of the children—Oliver—who slowly picks up his bowl, rises, and hesitantly approaches Mr. Bumble. (It seems that Oliver has been selected as a representative of the children to request more food!) Everyone waits and watches in silence as Oliver asks for *more to eat!* Mr. Bumble goes into a furious rage and calls for his helpers to seize Oliver and lock him up!

• F O R   S T U D Y •

Can you provide background music or appropriate sounds during or following the preceding narration? Remember that your music must enhance or add to the drama, the expressiveness, and the excitement. Weave your music between the narration; do not overpower or drown out the speaker.

NARRATOR 2: Before the second scene, Mr. Bumble and Widow Corney have decided that Oliver is a troublemaker and plan to get rid of him. With his belongings wrapped in a small bundle, Oliver is led onto the streets by Mr. Bumble, who hawks him for sale to the highest bidder.

Boy for Sale (Mr. Bumble)

SCENE 2

SETTING: *The upper level has a door with a sign reading Sowerberry Funeral Home. The lower level is a funeral workroom with coffins, bucket, mop, scrub brush, and a dog's bowl.*

· FOR STUDY ·

Can you prepare music for this scene, to be included before the song "Where Is Love"? How will you express musically Oliver's feelings in this situation? Which instruments will best provide the mood? In which direction should the melodic line move? Consider the tempo, dynamic levels, and rhythm patterns of your composition.

NARRATOR 1: Eventually Mr. Sowerberry, an undertaker, who is in need of an assistant, decides to take Oliver on a trial basis. He is assured by Mr. Bumble that Oliver will require very little food and will work hard for his keep. Sowerberry immediately puts Oliver to work, gives him the remains of food in the dog's bowl as his meal, and sends him to the downstairs room where coffins are stored. *(Oliver's song, "Where is Love?", on page 222, is the theme and essence of the Dickens novel. Oliver reflects on his search for love.)*

Where Is Love?

Words and Music by Lionel Bart

Oliver

Where _____ is love? Does it fall from skies a-

bove? Is it un - der - neath the wil - low tree _____ that

I've been dream - ing of? Where _____ is she,

Who I close my eyes to see? Will I ev - er know that

sweet "hel - lo" _____ that's meant for on - ly me?

Who can say where she may hide? Must I tra - vel far and wide,

Till I am be - side the some - one who I can mean

some - thing to? Where, _____ where _____ is

poco rit.   *a tempo*

love? Who can say where she may hide?

Must I tra - vel far and wide, Till I am be - side the some-one who I can mean some-thing to? Where, where is love?

NARRATOR 2: Noah Claypole, a bully, who also works for Mr. Sowerberry, provokes Oliver into a fight by taunting him about his mother. To subdue him, Mrs. Sowerberry and her daughter, Charlotte, throw Oliver into a coffin. This upsets Mrs. Sowerberry and causes her to faint. As the others rush to Mrs. Sowerberry's aid, Oliver manages to escape from the undertaking establishment and moves toward another episode in his life.

SCENE 3

SETTING: *Fagin's den on one side, a road to London on other side of stage.*

NARRATOR 1: Alone, hungry, and friendless, Oliver has spent several days and nights on the roads leading to London. As he pauses on his journey to rest and finish the remains of a crust of bread, he is closely observed by an outlandishly dressed young man named Jack Dawkins, better known as the Artful Dodger. Dodger approaches Oliver, offers him an apple and an introduction to his boss, Fagin, who (he promises) will give Oliver food, a job, and a place to sleep.

Oliver finds it hard to believe that he has found a friend, as Dodger assures him that he will be welcomed as one of the family. Perhaps Oliver is finally about to experience a turn for the better. Come with him now to discover if the change *is* for the better . . . or for the worse.

Consider Yourself

Words and Music by Lionel Bart

lar - der days, why grouse? Al - ways a chance we'll meet

some - bo - dy to foot the bill, Then the drinks are on the

house! ___ Con - si - der your-self our mate. We

don't want to have no fuss, For af - ter some con -

si - der - a - tion we can state: Con - si - der your-self one of

Oliver   *Dodger*

us! Con - si - der your-self at home, ___ Con -

Oliver   *Dodger*

si - der your - self one of the fa - mi - ly. We've

Oliver   *Dodger*   *Both*

ta - ken to you so strong. It's clear we're

Dodger   *Oliver*

go - ing to get a - long. Con - si - der your - self well

(All move to Fagin's den at close of song.)

· FOR STUDY ·

Can you compose an appropriate theme or motive to be played whenever Fagin appears or is referred to in the narration? Remember, there is a tinge of humor and a theatrical flair in this devious criminal!

NARRATOR 2: Once inside Fagin's den, as his abode is so aptly named, Oliver is introduced to Fagin, the sly and crafty older gentleman who runs a school for pickpockets and thieves. Oliver's interest in Fagin's "business" (which to this point has not been explained to Oliver) prompts Fagin and his students to describe their work through song and pantomime. Oliver is even given a chance to "try his hand" at their profession during this musical number.

LISTENING LIBRARY

You've Got to Pick a Pocket or Two

NARRATOR 1: When everyone has been fed and bedded down for the night, Fagin brings from a secret hiding place a chest filled with expensive jewels that he has managed to keep aside for himself. He delights in holding each piece and admiring its beauty. He revels in the fortune he has amassed for himself, and he feels the jewels may be his insurance for his later years or against unforeseen problems.

• FOR STUDY •

You may want to consider segments (or all) of "Fagin's Theme" interspersed throughout the above narration as an underscore.

NARRATOR 2: The next morning, everyone is aroused when Nancy and Bet arrive. Both are involved in Fagin's business. In addition, Nancy works as a waitress and is the girlfriend of Bill Sikes, who is feared and hated by all. Nancy is introduced to the new boy, Oliver, and immediately senses that his manners mark him as different from the rest. Here is a young gentleman!

NARRATOR 1: Nancy and Dodger—both of whom love to be on stage and have a definite flair for drama—decide they will show the group how proper ladies and gentlemen should act as they put on their airs of upper-crust society for all. *(Nancy and Dodger sing "I'd Do Anything," on page 230.)*

I'd Do Anything

Words and Music by Lionel Bart

Dodger
I'd do an-y-thing for you, dear,

an-y-thing, for you mean ev-'ry-thing to me! ___

___ I know that I'd go an-y-where for your smile,

an-y-where, for your smile ev-'ry-where I'd see. ___

Nancy Would you climb a hill? *Dodger* An-y-thing! *Nancy* Wear a

daf-fo-dil? *Dodger* An-y-thing! *Nancy* Leave me all your will?

Dodger An-y-thing! *Nancy* Ev-en fight my Bill? *Dodger* What, fist-i-cuffs?

I'd risk ev-'ry-thing for one kiss, ev-'ry-thing, Yes,

Nancy *Dodger*
I'd do an-y-thing! An-y-thing? An-y-thing for you!

NARRATOR 2: Within a few days, Oliver is sent off into the streets with Dodger to observe how successful pickpocketing is accomplished.

Outside a bookstore, Dodger skillfully removes a wallet from a wealthy gentleman's pocket.

Almost instantly the man realizes that his wallet is missing as he reaches to pay for a purchase.

Dodger makes a quick exit from the scene and the gentleman turns to see Oliver, looking both innocent and guilty at once.

Oliver hesitates, gathers his wits, and runs. He is thought to be the thief and is captured as Act One concludes.

ACT II, SCENE 1

Oom Pah Pah

NARRATOR 1: As Act Two begins, Nancy is entertaining her customers with a rousing song, "Oom Pah Pah!". All join her as they beat time, move to the music, sing heartily, and applaud loudly.

NARRATOR 2: Suddenly the jovial atmosphere is hushed as everyone cowers and tries to hide in the shadows. Bill Sikes has entered the room! He brags of his brute strength and evil ways. He dares anyone to move or speak as he saunters about the room!

NARRATOR 1: The spell is broken as a breathless Dodger rushes in to inform Fagin, Sikes, and Nancy of Oliver's capture. He also relates that during the court trial, the bookseller who observed the crime absolved Oliver of any wrongdoing.

NARRATOR 2: And the wealthy gentleman, Mr. Brownlow, victim of the crime, has taken Oliver with him to his home!

NARRATOR 1: Both Sikes and Fagin realize that Oliver may talk and expose their operation to the law. They determine that Oliver must be taken from his benefactor. As their thoughts turn to who might best accomplish this deed, Sikes decides that Nancy could pull it off because Oliver trusts her friendship.

NARRATOR 2: When Nancy refuses and pleads that Oliver deserves this chance for a better life, Sikes strikes her and threatens to kill her.

NARRATOR 1: Left alone, Nancy sings a soliloquy that reveals her innermost feelings for Sikes and her need to love and be loved in return. *("As Long as He Needs Me," page 234)*

· FOR STUDY ·

Although the above narration is fast-moving, exciting, and loaded with conflicting emotions, it is lengthy. Here is an opportunity to incorporate music, sounds, or themes you have already composed or to add new music. Your music may occur within a narrator's segment or between narrations.

As Long as He Needs Me

Words and Music by Lionel Bart

As long as he needs me, ___ I know where I must be; ___ I'll cling on stead - fast - ly, ___ as long as he needs me. ___ Who else would love him still, ___ when they'd been used so ill? ___ He knows I al - ways will, ___ as long as he needs me. ___ If you are lone - ly, ___ then you will know, ___ when some - one needs you, ___ you love them so! ___ I won't be - tray his trust, ___ Tho' peo-ple say I must, ___ I've got to stay true just ___ as long as he needs me!

SCENE 2

SETTING: *The lower level represents a street. The upper level shows the doorway entrance to Mr. Brownlow's house.*

(Vendors appear on the street with baskets of flowers, fruits, vegetables, pails of milk, and so on. Mr. Brownlow and Oliver stand at the doorway, observing.)

NARRATOR 2: At the Brownlow residence, Oliver is under excellent care, is in good health, is receiving an education, has fine clothing, and—finally—is loved.

NARRATOR 1: (A most interesting point to note at this time: Mr. Brownlow cannot remove from his mind the striking resemblance between Oliver and his own daughter, Agnes, who vanished approximately ten years ago).

NARRATOR 2: One beautiful day, Mr. Brownlow decides to send Oliver to the library to return some books. Everyone is caught up in the joy of this song as Oliver unknowingly walks into the trap Nancy has set for him. *("Who Will Buy?" page 236)*

Who Will Buy?

Words and Music by Lionel Bart

Rose Seller

Who will buy my sweet red ros - es, two __ blooms for a

pen - ny? Who will buy my sweet red ros - es, two __ blooms for a

pen - ny?

Milkmaid

Will you buy an - y milk to - day,

Who will

mis - tress? An - y milk to - day, mis - tress?

buy my sweet red ros - es?

An - y milk to - day,

From the Columbia Pictures-Romulus Film OLIVER! © Copyright 1960 Lakeview Music Co., Ltd., London, England. TRO—Hollis Music, Inc., New York, controls all publication rights for the U.S.A. and Canada. Used by permission.

sky you ne-ver did see! ___ Who will tie it up with a rib-

All

-bon, and put it in a box for me? There'll nev-er

be a day so sun-ny, _____ It could not hap-pen twice.

Where is the man with all the mon-ey? _____ It's cheap at

half the price! ____ Who will buy this won-der-ful morn - ing?

I'm so high, I swear I could fly. ____ Me, oh my! I

Oliver Moderately

don't want to lose ___ it! So what am I to do, to

keep the sky so blue? There must be some-one who will buy!

Rose Seller

Who will buy my sweet red ros - es, two _ blooms for a pen-ny?

(At the end of the song, when the rose seller sings, Oliver begins to walk down the street. Nancy and Bet appear as Oliver innocently greets them.)

NARRATOR 1: Nancy pretends that Oliver is her lost brother, who ran away from home and broke his mother's heart. Her acting is so convincing that the crowd turns against Oliver and ignores his pleas that the whole scene is a sham.

NARRATOR 2: Sikes appears and he and Nancy hustle Oliver away to Fagin's hideout. Kidnapped! Once again, Oliver's life has taken a drastic turn!

SCENE 3:

SETTING: *Fagin's den. Nancy, Sikes, Oliver, Dodger, Fagin. Nancy standing apart from others, Sikes roughly holding Oliver, Dodger alongside Fagin. When narration concludes, Nancy angrily moves off, followed by Sikes pushing Oliver. Finally, Dodger walks off in same direction, leaving Fagin alone on stage.)*

NARRATOR 1: Nancy is upset over her role in the kidnapping of Oliver and is concerned with Sikes's rough treatment of the boy. She informs Fagin and Sikes that she will tell all she knows of their operation if they are not careful. Once Nancy parts from their company, Fagin warns Sikes to watch her closely.

NARRATOR 2: When Sikes is out of earshot, Fagin orders Dodger to follow him. (Fagin has never trusted Sikes. Even though they work together, they are mortal enemies.)

NARRATOR 1: Now alone, Fagin brings out his chest of jewels and contemplates this latest turn of events. In his song, he ponders what he now must consider for his own way of life . . . even a change to going honest!

When Fagin sends Dodger off to follow Sikes and stands alone with his chest of jewels, try using Fagin's theme as an underscore.

Reviewing the Situation

Words and Music by Lionel Bart

NARRATOR 2: Meanwhile, back to the subplot in this adventure story. An old woman, Sally, who was present in the workhouse when a child was born to an inmate, has decided to unfold her long-kept secret to Mr. Bumble and Widow Corney before her death. (By the way, Mrs. Corney is now *Mrs. Bumble*!) Sally shows the locket she robbed from the child's dead mother and says that the dying woman's last words told of an inheritance for her child whose name was . . . *Oliver*!

NARRATOR 1: Mr. and Mrs. Bumble, in their greed, scheme to reclaim Oliver and thereby inherit his fortune for themselves. But Mr. Brownlow foils their plot when he becomes incensed over their treatment and sale of Oliver and threatens to have both of them fired from their positions. Upon opening the locket, Mr. Brownlow discovers that it contains a picture of his daughter Agnes. *He* is *Oliver's grandfather!*

NARRATOR 2: As the plot moves to a close, Nancy appears at Mr. Brownlow's residence and promises to bring Oliver to him at midnight on London Bridge.

(A bell strikes twelve times.)

NARRATOR 1: That night, as Nancy hurries Oliver to the appointed meeting, Bill Sikes stealthily follows and kills her. Mr. Brownlow appears just in time to see Sikes disappear with Oliver.

NARRATOR 2: As an angry crowd searches for Sikes, it batters in the door of Fagin's den, where Sikes has taken Oliver. Sikes pulls his hostage onto the roof in a desperate attempt to escape. He is discovered by the crowd, is shot, and falls to his death.

NARRATOR 1: In the meantime, Fagin and his pickpockets have been alerted and have managed to run to safety. The crowd emerges from Fagin's den, excitedly showing off his chest of precious jewels that it has uncovered. Oliver's grandfather, Mr. Brownlow, rescues Oliver and takes him home.

NARRATOR 2: Slowly, cautiously, from beneath the bridge where he has been hiding, Fagin emerges. Alone and contemplating his future once again, Fagin walks off as he sings: "Can somebody change? S'possible. Maybe it's strange—s'possible. All my dearest companions and treasures, I've left 'em behind. I'll turn a leaf over, and, who can tell what I may find?" Just before he exits, he turns toward us with a sly wink, a wry smile . . . and then disappears.

Finale—entire cast.

· FOR STUDY ·

A **reprise** of "Consider Yourself" and "I'd Do Anything" is suggested as the finale. You may prefer to arrange your own finale, coordinating music with the entrance of characters as they take curtain calls.

Audiences have fun in the theater. They laugh uproariously at the jokes and listen attentively to the songs, often applauding a song just as in an opera. If the dialogue is especially witty, they may even applaud that, as well.

Young Person's Guide to the Orchestra, "Introduction"
.... Britten

As you listen to the introduction to *Young Person's Guide to the Orchestra,* you will hear numbers called. At each number, look at the choice of answers. Circle the answer you think is correct.

1. Full orchestra   Clarinet and flute duet

2. Brass   Woodwinds

3. Organ   Brass

4. Strings   Drum

5. Percussion   Strings

6. Solo flute   Full orchestra

TEST 10

Write the letter of the correct answer in the blank.

1. When you listened to *Johnny Has Gone for a Soldier* you heard a folk singer accompanying herself on the mountain _____.

   a. flute   b. oboe
   c. dulcimer   d. recorder

2. A group of people performing together is called _____.

   a. an ensemble   b. a folk group
   c. a rock band   d. a music club

3. A song for two vocal parts is called _____.

   a. a trio   b. a symphony
   c. a choir   d. a duet

4. A song for three vocal parts is called _____.

   a. a trio   b. a symphony
   c. a choir   d. a duet

5. The Hi-Los, a men's vocal group, use a kind of harmony called _____.

   a. right harmony   b. close harmony
   c. real harmony   d. instrumental harmony

6. A large group of voices is called _____.

   a. a solo   b. a chorus
   c. an orchestra   d. a flutist

TEST 11

Write the letter of the correct answer in the blank.

1. You learned that instruments are grouped in families. The violin is a part of the _____ family.

   a. woodwind   b. string
   c. brass   d. percussion

2. The flute is a member of the _____ family.

   a. woodwind   b. string
   c. brass   d. percussion

3. The bass drum is a member of the _____ family.

   a. woodwind   b. string
   c. brass   d. percussion

4. The trumpet is a member of the _____ family.

   a. woodwind   b. string
   c. brass   d. percussion

5. The clarinet is a member of the _____ family.

   a. woodwind   b. string
   c. brass   d. percussion

6. The cymbals are a member of the _____ family.

   a. woodwind   b. string
   c. brass   d. percussion

7. The trombone is a member of the _____ family.

   a. woodwind   b. string
   c. brass   d. percussion

8. The cello is a member of the _____ family.

   a. woodwind   b. string
   c. brass   d. percussion

TEST 12

Write the letter of the correct answer in the blank.

1. Many groups of people have special instruments. The Yoruba, of Africa, play a great deal on _____ .

   a. bagpipes   b. percussion instruments
   c. guitars   d. flutes

2. Steel drums are associated with the people of _____ .

   a. New England   b. Japan
   c. the West Indies   d. New York City

3. An ensemble of musicians in Mexico that includes guitars, trumpets, and violins is called _____ .

   a. a mariachi band   b. the Mexico City Philharmonic
   c. the Latin American Ensemble   d. the Mexico Group

4. The instrument most closely associated with Scotland is _____ .

   a. the bagpipe   b. the snare drum
   c. the guitar   d. the flute

5. In New Orleans a style of jazz was developed called _____ .

   a. hot   b. New York-style
   c. Dixieland   d. St. Louis

TEST 13

Write the letter of the correct answer in the blank.

1. A modern style that reduces harmony and melody to simple repetition is called _____ .

   a. neo-Baroque
   c. minimalism
   b. expressionism
   d. impressionism

2. The music that shows all the instruments or voices of a composition is called a _____ .

   a. line
   c. staff
   b. page
   d. score

3. Orchestra scores can be very complicated looking on the page. Often each instrument will have its own staff. If there are 18 different instruments, there will be _____ .

   a. an intermission
   c. 18 staffs
   b. two conductors
   d. three flutists

4. Because other instruments were added to the Baroque string orchestra, their parts are always notated _____ the strings.

   a. above
   b. below

5. In her interview, conductor Eve Queler places a great deal of importance to a conductor on _____ .

   a. reading books
   c. training
   b. traveling
   d. singers

TEST 14

Circle T if the statement is true; circle F if the statement is false.

1. *Oliver* is based on the story of Oliver Twist, by William Shakespeare.

    T   F

2. In Act I, the orphans are living in a palatial estate.

    T   F

3. The first song they sing is "Food, Glorious Food."

    T   F

4. Mr. Bumble sells Oliver to Mr. Sowerberry, an undertaker.

    T   F

5. Oliver escapes from Mr. Sowerberry and meets a boy called the Artful Codger.

    T   F

6. After being taken into Fagin's "business" Oliver is befriended by a young woman named Nancy, who is Fagin's girlfriend.

    T   F

7. Oliver is taken in by a wealthy gentleman, but is kidnapped by Bill Sikes.

    T   F

8. After Oliver's capture, Bill Sikes is chased onto a roof with Oliver and is allowed to go free.

    T   F

All for the Best

from *Godspell*

Words and Music by Stephen Schwartz

When you feel sad or un - der a curse, your life is bad, your pros - pects are worse, Your wife is sigh - ing, cry - ing, and your ol - ive tree is dy - ing. Tem - ples are grey - ing and teeth are de - cay - ing and cred - i - tors weigh - ing your purse! Your mood _ and your robe are both _ a deep blue. You'd bet that Job had noth - ing on you. Don't for - get that when you go to heav - en you'll be blessed, Yes, it's all for the best.

1. When you feel sad or un - der a
2. Some men are born to live at ease do - ing what they please, rich - er than the

America

Words by Samuel Francis Smith   Traditional Melody

1. My coun - try! 'tis of thee, Sweet land of
2. My na - tive coun - try, thee, Land of the
3. Let mu - sic swell the breeze, And ring from
4. Our fa - ther's God, to thee, Au - thor of

lib - er - ty, Of thee I sing; Land where my
no - ble free, Thy name I love; I love thy
all the trees, Sweet free - dom's song; Let mor - tal
lib - er - ty, To thee we sing; Long may our

fa - thers died, Land of the Pil - grims' pride,
rocks and rills, Thy woods and tem - pled hills,
tongues a - wake, Let all that breathe par - take,
land be bright with free - dom's ho - ly light,

From ev - 'ry___ moun - tain - side, Let___ free - dom ring!
My heart___ with___ rap - ture thrills Like___ that a - bove.
Let rocks___ their___ si - lence break, The___ sound pro - long.
Pro - tect___ us___ by thy might, Great___ God, our King!

Dona nobis pacem

Words Traditional   Music by Allen Brings

Theme

1. Do - na____ no -

Theme in diminution (shorter notes)

2. Do - na____ no - bis____ pa - cem, Do -

1. bis____ pa - cem, Do -

2. na____ no - bis pa - cem, Do - na____

Erie Canal

American Folk Song

al - ways know your neigh - bor, You'll al - ways know your pal, If you

ev - er nav - i - gat - ed on the E - rie Ca - nal. ___

Gaudeamus omnes in Domino

Plainsong

Gau - de - a - mus om - nes _ in _ Do - mi - no, ___
gow - day - ah - moos ohm - nehs een doh - mee - noh

di - em _ fe - stum ___ ce - le - bran - tes ___ sub hon - o - re ___
dee - ehm feh - stoom cheh - leh - brahn - tehs soob ohn - oh - reh

sanc - to - rum ___ om - ni - um: de _ quo - rum sol - em - ni - ta -
sahnk - toh - room ohm - nee - oom day qwoh - room sohl - ehm - nee - tah -

te _ gau - dent An - ge - li, ___ et col - lau -
teh gow - dehnt ahn - geh - lee eht kohl - low -

dant _ Fi - li - um _____ De - i.
dahnt fee - lee - oom day - ee

Here We Come A-Singing

Words and Music by David Eddleman

Here we come a-sing-ing the fes-ti-val of lights, sing-ing of a lamp that
Hap-py times are here for the peo-ple ev'-ry-where; laugh-ing voi-ces sing-ing

burned eight nights;
here and there;
Spin the drey-dl, light the me-nor-ah, sing of the he-ro's fight.

gifts from the ones who care. Cel-e-brate the vic-to-ry time, cel-e-brate with

sing-ing and rhyme; Cel-e-brate the sto-ry they told of the eight-day

mir-a-cle of old. Fes-ti-val of sing-ing and fes-ti-val of joy,

cheer-ing ev-'ry hap-py girl and boy; Spin the drey-dl,

light the me-nor-ah, time that we all en-joy.

He's Got the Whole World in His Hands

African-American Spiritual

Guitar: capo 3

1. He's got the whole world ___ in his hands, ___
2. He's got the wind and rain ___ in his hands, ___
3. He's got both you and me ___ in his hands, ___

He's got the whole world ___ in his hands, ___
He's got the wind and rain ___ in his hands, ___
He's got both you and me ___ in his hands, ___

He's got the whole world ___ in his hands, ___
He's got the wind and rain ___ in his hands, ___
He's got both you and me ___ in his hands, ___

He's got the whole world in his hands. _____
He's got the whole world in his hands. _____
He's got the whole world in his hands. _____

Hosanna

Calypso Song from Jamaica

1. Ho - san - na, me build a house, __ oh, _ Ho - san - na, me build a house, __ oh, _ Ho -
2. Ho - san - na, me build a house, __ oh, _ Ho - san - na, me build a house, __ oh, _ Ho -

san - na, me build a house, __ oh, _ I built it on the sand - y ground. _
san - na, me build a house, __ oh, _ I build it on the sol - id ground. _

Solo

Me house built on _ a sand - y ground. _ It will fall, you see. Me
Me house built on _ a sol - id ground. _ It'll stand up, you see. Me

house built with sand all 'round. _ It will fall, you see.
house built on sol - id ground. _ It'll stand up, you see.

The rain _ will _ wet it up, Ha! Ha! The sun will burn it _ up, Ha! Ha! The
The rain _ can't _ wet it up, Ha! Ha! The sun can't burn it _ up, Ha! Ha! The

breeze will shake it _ up, Ha! Ha! The storm come blow it _ down, Ha! Ha! Me
breeze can't shake it _ up, Ha! Ha! The storm can't blow it _ down, Ha! Ha! Me

house can nev - er _ be, No! No! Me house too weak, you _ see, No! No! Me
house will ev - er _ be, Yes! Yes! Me house too strong, you _ see, Yes! Yes! Me

house will not stand, No! _ No! _ Storm blow it on - to the ground, Ha! Ha!
house will ever stand, Yes! _ Yes! _ Storm can't _ bring it to ground, Ha! Ha!

I Like It Here

Words and Music by Clay Boland

I like the U - nit - ed States of A - mer - i - ca, ____
I am so luck - y to be in A - mer - i - ca, ____

I like the way we all live with - out fear; ____
And I am thank - ful each day of the year, ____

I like to vote for my choice, ____ speak my mind, raise my voice,
For I can do as I please, ____ 'cause I'm free as the breeze,

1.
Yes, I like it here. ____

2.
like it here.

I'd like to climb to the top of a moun - tain so high, ____

Lift my head to the sky ____ and say how grate - ful am I ____

For the way that I'm liv - ing, I'm work - ing and giv - ing

And help - ing the land I hold dear, ____ Yes,

I like it, I like it, I like it here. ____

I Love Pasta

Words and Music by Sol Berkowitz

I Love the Mountains

Traditional

Guitar: capo 5

I F C — Dm Am — Gm Dm — C₇ G₇

I love the moun - tains, I love the roll - ing hills,

II F C — Dm Am — Gm Dm — C₇ G₇

I love the flow - ers, I love the daf - fo - dils,

III F C — Dm Am — Gm Dm — C₇ G₇

I love the fire - side When all the lights are low,

IV F C — Dm Am — Gm Dm — C₇ G₇

Boom - de - ah - da, boom - de - ah - da, Boom - de - ah - da, boom - de - ah - da.

(Last time: Voice I sings the last phrase, "Boom-de-ah-da," etc. four times, Voice II sings this phrase three times, Voice III twice, Voice IV once, then all sing the Coda together.)

Coda F C — 3 — C₇ G₇ — F C

Boom did - dle - dee - dum - dum, Boom, boom.

If

Words and Music by David Gates

If a pic-ture paints a thou-sand words, then why can't I paint you?
man could be two plac-es at one time, I'd be with you

The words will nev-er show the you I've come to know.
to-mor-row and to-day, be-side you all the way.

If a face could launch a thou-sand ships, then where am I to go?
If the world should stop re-volv-ing, spin-ning slow-ly down to die,

There's no one home but you. You're all that's left me,
I'd spend the end with you. And when the world was

too. And when my love for life is run-ning dry, you
through, then one by one the stars would all go out. Then

1.
come and pour your-self on me. If a
you and I would

2. *rit.*
sim-ply fly a-way.

Jolly Old Saint Nicholas

Traditional

1. Jol-ly old Saint Ni-cho-las, Lean your ear this way. Don't you tell a

sin-gle soul What I'm going to say; Christ-mas Eve is com-ing soon,

Now, you dear old man, Whis-per what you'll bring to me, Tell me if you can.

2. When the clock is striking twelve,
   When I'm fast asleep,
   Down the chimney tall and round,
   With your pack you'll creep;
   All the stockings you will find
   Hanging in a row;
   Mine will be the shortest one,
   You'll be sure to know.

3. Johnny wants a pair of skates,
   Susie wants a toy,
   Nancy wants a story book,
   One to bring her joy;
   As for me, I'm not too sure,
   So I'll say "goodnight,"
   Choose for me, dear Santa Claus,
   What you think is right.

Mangwani Mpulele

Zulu Folk Song   Adapted by Theodore Bikel

Mang - wa - ni mpu - le - le ki-nel-wa ki - tu - la. (a mang-wa-ni)
mahng - wah-nee mpoo - lay-lay kee-nehl-wah kee-too - lah (ah mahng-wah-nee)

Mang - wa - ni mpu - le - le ki-nel-wa ki - tu - la. Le -
mahng - wah-nee mpoo - lay-lay kee-nehl-wah kee-too - lah lay -

hae-le mu-la,   le hae-le mu-le   ki-nel-wa ki-tu - la. (a mang-wa-ni) Le -
high-lay moo-lah   *lay high-lay moo-lay*   *kee-nehl-wah kee-too - lah (ah mahng-wah-nee) lay-*

hae-le mu-la,   le hae-le mu-le   ki-nel-wa ki-tu - la. (a mang-wa-ni)
high-lay moo-lah   *lay high-lay moo-lay*   *kee-nehl-wah kee-too - lah ah mahng-wah-nee*

la.   Mang - wa-ni   mpu - le-le   ki-nel-wa ki-tu -
mahng - wah-nee   mpoo - lay-lay   kee-nehl-wah kee-too -

la. (a mang-wa-ni) Mang - wa-ni   mpu - le-le   ki-nel-wa ki-tu - la.
lah (ah mahng-wah-nee) mahng - wah-nee   mpoo - lay-lay   kee-nehl-wah kee-too - lah

Mary Ann

Calypso Song from the West Indies

2. All day, all night, Miss Mary Ann,
   Down by the seashore sifting sand,
   Young and old, come join the band,
   Down by the seashore sifting sand.

3. All day, all night, Miss Mary Ann,
   Down by the seashore sifting sand,
   Ev'rybody come and join the band,
   Down by the seashore sifting sand.

The Mermaid

Traditional Sea Chantey

roll, (let 'em roll) And the storm-y winds may blow, (let 'em blow _____) But

we poor sai-lors go skip-ping to the top, While the land-lub-bers lie down be-

Fine

low, (be-low, be-low) While the land-lub-bers lie down be-low.

Slowly

3. Then three times a-round went our gal-lant_ ship, And three times a-round went

she. (went she) Then three times a-round went our gal-lant_ ship, And she

sank to the bot-tom of the sea,
(bot-tom of the sea)

D.S. al Fine

And she

sank to the bot-tom of the sea.

A Mighty Fortress Is Our God

Melody by Martin Luther   Harmonization by J. S. Bach
Translation by Frederick H. Hedge

1. A might-y for-tress is_ our God, A bul-wark nev-er_
2. That word a-bove_ all earth-ly powers, No thanks to them, a-

Noble Dame

Words and Music by Manos Hadjidakis and Dorian Rudnytsky   Arranged by Larry Eisman

1. She was a la - dy, once a no - ble name, No - ble Dame, ___
2. She was a la - dy, once with - out a care, gold - en hair, ___

She had a sil - ver ring from the king; ___
She was the on - ly friend of the king; ___

Give her a nick - el, take her out to dine, out __ to dine, ___
May - be she'll come and ask you for your name, no - ble dame, ___

Com - fort her if she sighs and then cries. ___
We'll give our love to her on her way. ___

Look for her by the foun - tain on the road, ___ say, __ "Hel-

lo," ___ Don't be a - fraid to smile and then go. ___

And if you see her talk - ing to her - self ___ all a-

lone, ___ Leave her a - lone her heart is at home. ___

One Tin Soldier

Guitar: capo 2

Words and Music by Dennis Lambert and Brian Potter

1. Lis - ten, chil - dren, to a sto - ry that was writ - ten long a - go,
2. So the peo - ple of the val - ley sent a mes - sage up the hill
3. Now the val - ley cried with an - ger, "Mount your hors - es! Draw your sword!"

'Bout a king - dom on a moun - tain and the val - ley folk be - low;_
Ask - ing for_ the bur - ied treas - ure, tons of gold_ for which they'd kill.
And they killed_ the moun - tain peo - ple so they won_ their just re - ward._

On the moun - tain was a treas - ure bur - ied deep be - neath_ a stone,
Came an an - swer from the king - dom "with our broth - ers we_ will share
Now they stood_ be - side the treas - ure on the moun - tain, dark_ and red

And the val - ley peo - ple swore_ they'd have it for_ their ver - y
All the se - crets of our moun - tain, all the rich - es bur - ied
Turned the stone_ and looked be - neath_ it, "Peace on earth"_ was all it

REFRAIN

own.
there." Go a-head and hate your neigh - bor, _ go a-head and cheat_ a friend.
said.

Do it in the name of heav - en, _ jus - ti - fy it in _ the end. _ There

won't be an - y trum - pets blow - in' ___ come the judg - ment day; On the

blood - y morn - ing af - ter ___ one tin sol - dier rides a - way. ___

Puttin' On the Style

American Folk Song   New Words and New Music Adaptation by Norman Cazden

REFRAIN

Put-tin' on the ag-o-ny, put-tin' on the style, That's what all the

young folks are do-in' all the while. And as I look a-round me, I'm

ver-y apt to smile To see so man-y peo-ple put-tin' on the style. *Fine*

VERSE

1. Young man in a car-riage, ___ driv-in' like ___ he's
2. Sweet six-teen and goes to school just ___ to see the
3. Young man home from col-lege ___ makes ___ a great dis-

mad, With a pair of hors-es ___ he bor-rowed from his
boys, Turns and laughs and gig-gles ___ at ev-'ry lit-tle
play, With a fan-cy ad-jec-tive that he can hard-ly

dad; He cracks his whip so live-ly just to watch his la-dy
noise; She turns this way a lit-tle, then ___ turns that way a-
say; It can't be found in Web-ster's, and it won't be for a-

D.C. al Fine

smile, ___ But she knows he's on-ly put-tin' on the style.
while, But we know that she's on-ly put-tin' on the style.
while, But ev-'ry-bod-y knows ___ he's put-tin' on the style.

Raisins and Almonds

Yiddish Words and Music by Abraham Goldfaden   English Words by David ben Avraham

Freely

In dem beys ha-mik-dosh, in a vin-kl chey-der, zitst di al-
ihn dehm bays hah-mihk-dohsh ihn a veen-k(uh)l khay-dehr zihtst dee ahl-
In midst of the vil-lage, there's a tem-ple so love-ly, In-side the

mo-ne, bas Tzi-on a-leyn. Ir ben yo-chi-dl, yi-de-len,
maw-nuh bahs tsee-awhn ah-layn. eer behn yoh-chee-d(uh)l yee-duh-lehn,
door sits a wi-dow a-lone. In the cra-dle she rocks lies her

vigt zi ki-sey-der, un zingt im tzum shlo-fn a li-de-le
vihgt zee kee-say-dehr oon zeenkt ihm tsoom shluh-f(oh)n a lih-duh-luh
ba-by a sleep-ing, and she lulls him to sleep with a sweet slum-ber

sheyn. "Un-ter yi-de-les vi-ge-le____ shteyt a klor veys
shayn oon-tehr yee-duh-luhs vee-guh-luh shtayt a klawr vays
song. "'Neath the cra-dle that holds__ your__ dream,__ stands a goat as

tsi-ge-le.____ Dos tsi-ge-le iz ge-fo-rn hand-len.__
tsee-guh-luh duhs tsee-guh-luh ihz guh-faw-r(uh)n hahnt-lehn
white__ as__ cream.__ The goat__ will be__ soon__ to mar-ket.__

__ Dos vet zayn dayn ba-ruf.____ Ro-zhin-kes__ mit
duhs veht zayn dayn bah-roof roh-zheen-kuhs miht
There a prom-ise to keep:____ To buy you rais-ins and

mand-len.____ Shlof-zhe, yi-de-le, shlof."____
mund-l(eh)n shluhf-zhuh yee-duh-luh shluhf
al-monds.__ Sleep, my lit-tle one, sleep."

Sakura

(Cherry Blossoms)

Japanese Folk Song   Arranged by Bruce Saylor

Scattin' with Solfège

Sol Berkowitz   Based on a Violin Study by Kreutzer

Sentimental Journey

Words and Music by Bud Green, Les Brown and Ben Homer

Guitar: capo 5

Gon - na take a sen - ti-men - tal jour-ney, Gon - na set my
Got my bag, I got my res - er-va - tion, Spent each dime I

heart at ease. _ Gon - na make a sen - ti-men - tal jour-ney, To re-new old
could af - ford. _ Like a child in wild an - ti - ci-pa-tion, Long to hear that

mem - o - ries. _ Sev - en, _ that's the time we leave, at sev - en. _
"All _ a - board." _

I'll be wait - in' up for Heav - en, _ Count - in' ev - 'ry mile of

rail-road track _ that takes me back. _ Nev - er thought my heart could be so "yearn-y."

Why did I de - cide to roam? _ Got - ta take this

sen - ti-men - tal jour-ney, sen - ti-men - tal jour - ney home. _

So My Sheep May Safely Graze

Words and Music by Rod McKuen

Guitar: capo 5

1. So my sheep may safe-ly graze_ I'd climb the high-est hill, ____ And
2. All good shep-herds watch their flocks_ to the low-est lamb ____
3. Last night there were sol-diers on _ the road ____ be-low the town ____ And

keep a watch ____ out for the hawk_ and for the howl-ing wolf. ____ I
So that they ____ may safe-ly graze_ and nev-er come to harm. ____
crea-tures _ in the heav-ens with_ wings ____ of shin-y gold. ____

made a friend out of the wind_ and got to know the snow. So
Guard-ed from the hunt-er's horn_ shield-ed from the sun.
One of them came close to me_ say-ing, "Do not be a-fraid. A

e-ven in the win-ter-time_ my sheep may safe-ly graze. ____
All my sheep may safe-ly graze_ in far fields or at home. ____ Call-ing,
child of God was born this night;_ Your sheep may safe-ly graze." ____

REFRAIN

"Come, sheep, come, I'll count you one by one.   One for John and one for Ja-cob,

"Come, sheep, come,   I'll count you one by one.   Ah ____

One for Job and one for the child who's born this morn-ing in Beth-le-hem."
(born _____)

And _ one for the child who's born in Beth - le - hem."

Spring Song

English Words by Theron Haithwaite   Music by Franz Joseph Haydn

The ear - ly spring-time breez-es blow - ing, Re -

fresh - ing ev - 'ry field and glade. _ To all the breath of life be -

stow - ing, The fra-grance in the cool-ing shade. _ We

won - der in the gift of spring - time, We cel - e-brate the length-'ning

days. We sing _ the _ song of earth's re - new - ing, And

hymn our _ grate-ful spi-rits' praise. We hymn our grate-ful spi-rits' praise.

The Star-Spangled Banner

Words by Francis Scott Key   **Music by John Stafford Smith**

1. Oh, ___ say! can you see by the dawn's ear - ly light,

What so proud - ly we hailed at the twi - light's last gleam - ing,

Whose broad stripes and bright stars, through the per - il - ous fight,

O'er the ram - parts we watched were so gal - lant - ly stream - ing?

And the rock - ets' red glare, the bombs burst - ing in air,

Gave proof through the night that our flag was still there.

Oh, say, does that ___ Star - Span - gled Ban - ner ___ yet ___ wave ___

O'er the land ___ of the free and the home of the brave.

2. On the shore, dimly seen through the mists of the deep,
   Where the foe's haughty host in dread silence reposes,
   What is that which the breeze, o'er the towering steep,
   As it fitfully blows, half conceals, half discloses?
   Now it catches the gleam of the morning's first beam,
   In full glory reflected now shines on the stream;
   'Tis the Star-Spangled Banner, oh, long may it wave
   O'er the land of the free and the home of the brave!

3. Oh, thus be it ever when free men shall stand
   Between their loved homes and the war's desolation!
   Blest with vict'ry and peace, may the heav'n-rescued land
   Praise the Pow'r that hath made and preserved us a nation!
   Then conquer we must, for our cause it is just,
   And this be our motto: "In God is our trust!"
   And the Star-Spangled Banner in triumph shall wave
   O'er the land of the free and the home of the brave!

Step to the Rear

from *How Now, Dow Jones*

Words by Carolyn Leigh   Music by Elmer Bernstein

Will ev-'ry one here __ kind-ly step to the rear __
__ And let a win-ner lead the way; _____
Here's where we sep - a - rate the notes from the noise, __ The
men from the boys, __ the rose from the poi - son i - vy.

Back in the bunch, __ I came up with a hunch, __ This was an
up and at 'em day; __ It's one of those spells __
__ when you hear the right bells __ And your hor - o-scope tells __
__ you to say. __ Will ev - 'ry - one here __
__ kind - ly step to the rear __ And let a win - ner
lead the way! __ I hear those trum - pets
be - gin to blare, __ And now I'm Wash - ing -
ton up - on the Del - a - ware. Will

Countermelody

Here he comes and things are

Melody

ev - 'ry - one here __ kind - ly step to the rear __

shows ya, Up on your toes ya

_ This was the time to rise and

can't go a - stray. So get in

say; _ I've got in my eye _

step be - hind a rep for

_ such a ju - bi - lant sky _ That the

vim and pep and sheer old fash - ioned

Fourth of Ju - ly _ will seem gray. _

guts and gump - tion, Cav - i - ar and

Will ev - 'ry - one here ___ kind - ly

pheas - ant for din - ner, A win - ner will lead the ___

step to the rear ___ And let a win - ner lead the

way, Just let a win - ner, let a win - ner, let a

way, Just let a win - ner

cool and crow - ing win - ner lead the way. ___

lead the way. ___

Thanksgiving Calypso

Words and Music by David Eddleman

1. Once a year __ we set a-side a day __ for cel-e-brat-ing in a
2. Say a thank-you for the air we breathe, __ the rain-y days __ a-mak-ing

spe-cial way, __ To count our bless-ings, count 'em by the score: the
shin-y leaves; __ The sun a-beam-ing on the gar-den wall __ is say-ing,

things we have __ to be thank-ful for. __ Let's sing a song of grat-i-
"Hap-py Thanks-giv-ing" to one and all. __ Let's sing a song of grat-i-

tude, Let's sing a song of hap-py days; We'll sing a thank-you song to

you, We'll sing a song of joy and praise. ___

Say, "Thank __ you" for the fields __ of grain, Say, "Thank __ you" for the fall-ing rain,

Say, "Thank __ you" for the chance __ to live in peace and har-mo-ny. ___

Time in a Bottle

Words and Music by Jim Croce

1. If I could save time in a bot - tle _____ The first thing that
2. If I could make days last for - ev - er, _____ If words could make
3. If I had a box just for wish - es _____ And dreams that had

I'd like to do _____ Is to save ev - 'ry day till e - ter - ni - ty
wish - es come true; _____ I'd save ev - 'ry day like a treas - ure and
nev - er come true; _____ The box would be emp - ty ex - cept for the

pass - es a - way Just to spend them with you. _____
then _____ a - gain I would spend them with you. _____
mem - 'ry of how they were an - swered by you. _____

But there nev - er seems to be e - nough time to do the things you

want to do once you find them. _____ I've

looked a - round e - nough to know that you're the one I

D.C. (3rd verse)
Fine

want to go through time with. _____

Tina Singu

Folk Song from Africa

Ti - na Sing - u, le - lu - vu - tae - o. Wat - sha, Wat - sha, Wat - sha.
tee - nah sing - oo lee - loo - voo - tye - oh waht - shah waht - shah waht - shah
We are burn - ing, burn - ing the fire; burn - ing, burn - ing, burn - ing.

Wat - sha, Wat - sha, Wat - sha, Wat - sha, Wat - sha.
waht - shah waht - shah waht - shah waht - shah waht - shah
Burn - ing, burn - ing, burn - ing, burn - ing, burn - ing.

La, la la la la la la, la la la la la la, la la la la la la la la la la.

From Chansons de Notre Chalet copyright © 1957 by World Around Songs

Try to Remember

from *The Fantasticks*

Words by Tom Jones   Music by Harvey Schmidt   Countermelody by Alan Seale

Guitar:

Countermelody (2nd time only)

1 Ah _____ Sep - tem - ber when life was

2 Try to re - mem - ber the kind of Sep - tem - ber when life was

1 slow and oh, so mel - low, ___ Ah _____

2 slow and oh, so mel - low. ___ Try to re - mem - ber the

Wi Yo He Yo

American Indian Song

Transcribed from the Library of Congress recording AFSL36.

You've Got a Friend

Words and Music by Carole King

When you're down ____ and trou - bled, And you need ____ some love and care, ____
____ a - bove ____ you grows ____ dark ____ and full of clouds, _

____ And noth - in' ____ noth - in' is go - in' right, ____
____ And that ol' ____ north wind be - gins _ to blow, ____

Close your eyes _ and think of me, _ and soon I ____ will be there ____ To
Keep your head _ to - geth - er, ____ and call my _ name out loud; ____

bright - en up ____ e - ven your dark - est night. ____
Soon you'll hear _ me ____ knock - in' at ____ your door. ____ You just call _

____ out my ____ name, ____ and you know ____ wher - ev - er I am, _

____ I'll come run - nin' ____ to see you a - gain. ____

Win - ter, spring, sum - mer or fall, _____ All you have to do is call, ____

Last time to Coda ⊕ │1.

____ and I'll be ____ there. ____ You've got a friend. _____

If the sky ___ there. _____ Now

ain't it good to know that you've ___ got a friend, _ when peo-ple can be ___ so cold? _

___ They'll hurt ___ you, yes, and de - sert ___ you, and take your soul _ if you

D.S. al ✛ Coda

let them. Oh, but don't you let ___ them. You just call ___

✛ *Coda*

___ there _ yes, I ___ will, ___ You've got a friend. _____ You've got a

Repeat and fade

friend. _____ It's so good ___ to know you've got a

LEARNING TO PLAY GUITAR

The guitar and keyboards are the most popular instruments used by people for making music. The pages that follow will help you get started playing chords on the guitar as an accompanying instrument for singing. Later you might also wish to learn how to read notes or play solos on the guitar. You will find that playing together in ensembles with other instrumentalists is a satisfying musical experience.

ROCK-ROCK   *Richard Lindner*

● The Guitar

There are three basic types of guitars—nylon-string classical, acoustic steel-string, and electric. Learn the names of the parts.

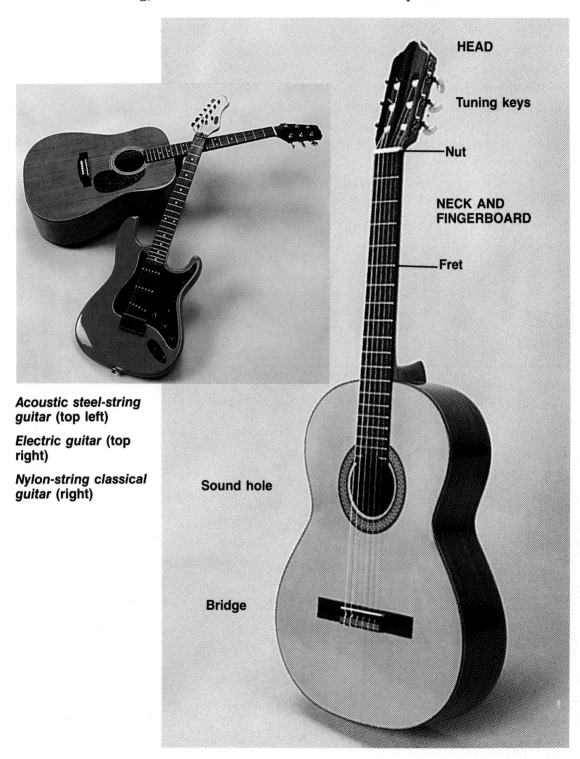

HEAD

Tuning keys

Nut

NECK AND FINGERBOARD

Fret

Sound hole

Bridge

Acoustic steel-string guitar (top left)

Electric guitar (top right)

Nylon-string classical guitar (right)

● Tuning

In the first stages of playing, your teacher may tune your guitar for you.

You can tune your guitar to the keys of a keyboard. The diagram below shows the pitches for tuning each guitar string. Another possibility is tuning to one of the inexpensive electronic guitar tuners. Still another way to tune is called *relative* tuning. When you are ready to tune your own guitar, follow the steps on page 309, and then have your teacher or an experienced guitar player check your accuracy.

middle C

E	A	D	G	B	E
6th string	5th string	4th string	3rd string	2nd string	1st string

Electronic guitar tuner

● How to Tune

- Tune the sixth, or lowest, string to E on the piano or pitch pipe.

- Press the sixth string at fret 5. This is the pitch A to which you tune your open fifth string. Pluck the depressed sixth string and the fifth string with your right thumb. When the two sounds match, you are in tune.

- Press the fifth string at fret 5, and tune the open fourth string to it. Follow the same procedure you used on the fifth and sixth strings.

- Press the fourth string at fret 5, and tune the open third string to it.

- Press the third string at fret 4, and tune the open second string to it.

- Press the second string at fret 5, and tune the open first string to it. Check the low E and the high E. They should be in tune with each other.

309

Playing Position

There are several ways to hold your guitar comfortably. The following guidelines will help you be a better player.

- Relax your muscles and avoid tension.
- The guitar neck should be either horizontal or tilted upwards (never down).
- Keep the body of the guitar as vertical as possible. Try not to slant the top of the guitar so you can see better. This puts your left hand in a bad position.

Left-hand fingers are numbered 1 through 4. (Pianists: The thumb is not number 1.) Place the thumb in back of the neck, and arch your fingers. Never hold the neck like a baseball bat with the palm against the back.

Your **right-hand thumb** will strum the strings by brushing across them in a downward motion.

The Capo

A **capo** (kay-po) is used to change keys on the guitar. When you see *Guitar: capo 3* on a song with guitar chords, place the capo at the third fret and play the chords printed in the contrasting color. You will finger the chords in a key that is easier to play on the guitar, but the resulting sound will match the key in which the song is notated.

Elastic capo

Capo in place at the third fret

How to Read Guitar Chord Diagrams

A guitar chord diagram shows you

- the **chord name**
- strings 6 (bass) through 1 (treble)
- the **nut**
- the **frets**
- left-hand fingers
- open (o) strings

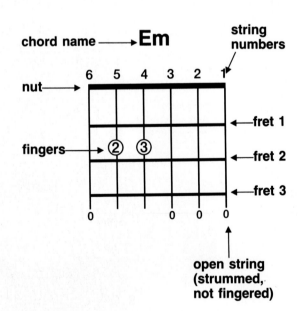

● The Em Chord

This diagram shows you how to play the E-minor chord.

Em

Strum strings 6 through 1. All strings should sound clear if you are pressing the strings firmly with the tips of the left-hand fingers. Arch your fingers so they touch only strings 4 and 5. Place your left thumb against the back of the neck.

You can accompany "Old Abram Brown," on page 99, with this one chord if you sing it in the key of E minor.

The songs "Shalom, Chaverim" and "Hey, Ho, Nobody Home" can also be played with the E-minor chord.

● The E Chord

This diagram shows you how to play the E-major chord.

E

To play the E-major chord, just add your first finger, pressing string 3 at the first fret. Strum strings 6 through 1. All strings should sound clear if you are playing on the tips of the fingers and pressing firmly.

Try the round "Frère Jacques" ("Are You Sleeping?"), which can be accompanied with the E-major chord.

● The E7 and A Chords

These chord diagrams show you how to play the E7 and A chords.

E₇

Strum the E7 chord from strings 6 through 1. Notice that the E7 chord is formed by lifting the third finger off string 4.

A

Strum strings 5 through 1. Arch your fingers and listen to be sure that string 1 is sounding, not dampened by the third finger. The x under string 6 tells you not to play that string. Watch for the x in other chord diagrams to follow.

The song "De colores," on page 130, uses these chords and is played in triple meter with three strums per measure. Practice this exercise; then sing and play the song, following the chord symbols above the music. In the exercise below, the strong beat (beat 1) is indicated by the chord symbol, and repeated strums on beats 2 and 3 are shown by the slashes.

$\frac{3}{4}$ A / / | A / / | E₇ / / | E₇ / / :‖

● The A7 and D Chords

These chord diagrams show you how to play the A7 and D chords.

A₇

Strum the A7 chord in a downward motion from strings 5 through 1. Do not play the bass string 6. Fingers 1 and 2 move as a unit from the A7 chord to the D chord. Practice moving them back and forth; then add the third finger on string 2 at the third fret to play the D chord.

D

Strum the D chord in a downward motion from strings 4 through 1. Do not play the bass strings 5 and 6. Arch your left-hand fingers and press the strings with the tip of the finger.

Strum this pattern with your right-hand thumb or pick. Move your left-hand fingers quickly as a unit to the new chord. Strum once for each letter and slash.

$\frac{4}{4}$ D / / ⸰ | A₇ / / ⸰ | D / / / | A₇ / / / :‖

You can use the A7 and D chords to accompany these songs in your book: "Mary Ann," page 275; "Water Come a Me Eye," page 84; "He's Got the Whole World in His Hands," page 263; "Elegua," page 13.

● A Three-Chord Song

Practice strumming this chord pattern in 4/4 meter. The chords are A, D, and E7.

$\frac{4}{4}$ A / / / | D / / / | A / / / | E₇ / / / :‖

Use these new chords to sing and strum these songs in your book: "The Marine's Hymn," page 99; "When the Saints Go Marching In," page 196. (Use A in place of A7, and D for Dm.)

● The Dm and Am Chords

Dm

Strum strings 4 through 1. Do not play strings 5 and 6. Arch your fingers, and listen to be sure that strings 2 and 1 are sounding. Remember to press the strings firmly.

Am

Strum strings 5 through 1. Practice moving from the Dm chord to the Am chord and back again until you can make the changes smoothly.

$\frac{4}{4}$ Dm / / / | Dm / / / | Am / / / | Am / / / :‖

$\frac{4}{4}$ Am / / / | Dm / / / | Am / / / | E₇ / / / :‖

Use these new chords to sing and strum these songs in your book: "Nine Hundred Miles," page 7 (Dm and Am); "Reviewing the Situation," page 240 (Dm and A7); "This Old Hammer," page 148 (Am, Dm, and E7); "Tumbalalaika," page 120 (Am, E, and Dm). (Because the meter changes from groups of three to groups of two, you will have to practice shifting the beat as you strum.)

● The G Chord

The G chord can be played several different ways. The top diagram shows the preferred fingering. The lower diagram shows a fingering for smaller hands.

Begin with a partial G chord using only one finger on string 1 and playing strings 4 through 1. Add the other fingers on strings 5 and 6 when you are ready.

G

Strum strings 4 through 1 for the partial G chord. Strum strings 6 through 1 for the full G chord. Arch your left-hand fingers and press the strings with the tip of the finger.

G

Strum strings 4 through 1 for the partial G chord. Strum strings 6 through 1 for the full G chord. For another alternate fingering, substitute the fourth finger for the third.

Strum and keep the beat steady.

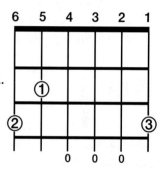

$\frac{4}{4}$ D / / 𝄽 | G / / 𝄽 | D / / 𝄽 | A₇ / / 𝄽 :‖

You can use D, A7, and G chords to accompany these songs in your book: "On My Journey," page 170; "This Land Is Your Land," page 114; "Rock Around the Clock," page 158 (use D and G in place of D7 and G7); "Oh, Susanna," page 151 (use traditional rhythm); "Laredo," page 186.

Other songs that use the G chord are "Glee Reigns in Galilee," page 200 (Em and G); "My White Horse," page 118 (Am, G, and E); "You Are My Sunshine," page 21 (D, G, A7, and E7).

● The G7 and D7 Chords

G₇

Start playing the G7 chord as a partial chord using only the first finger and strumming strings 4 through 1. Add the second and third fingers on strings 5 and 6 when you are ready. Notice how easy it is to change from the G chord.

D₇

Strum the D7 chord from strings 4 through 1. Do not play bass strings 5 and 6. Notice the triangle shape of this chord.

Go back and play "Rock Around the Clock," on page 158, using the G7 and D7 chords.

● Strum Variations

Try subdividing the beat by strumming both down and up. The symbol for a **down strum** is ⊓, and the symbol for an **up strum** is ∨.

Down up   Down up   Down up   Down up

● The C and F Chords

C

Strum strings 5 through 1. Do not play string 6. Arch your fingers and listen to be sure that strings 4, 3, and 1 are sounding. When you move from C to Am or D7 hold down any fingers that the chords have in common.

F

Strum strings 4 through 1. This chord uses a partial first finger bar that depresses strings 1 and 2. The F chord will be easier if you bring your left elbow in and roll the first finger slightly. Don't expect this chord to sound good right away. Lifting up your third finger will give you a Dm7 chord.

$\frac{4}{4}$ G / / / | Em / / / | C / / / | D₇ / / / :‖

$\frac{4}{4}$ C / / / | Am / / / | Dm / / / | G₇ / / / :‖

(or F)

Use the C chord with other chords you know to sing and strum these songs: "Puttin' On the Style," page 280 (C and G7); "I Love the Mountains," page 269 (C, Am, Dm, and G7); "I'd Like to Teach the World to Sing," page 107 (G, C, D, and A7); "Those Magic Changes," page 161 (G, Em, C, and D7); "Where Have All the Flowers Gone?" page 28 (G, Em, Am, C, and D7).

Use the F chord with other chords you know to play and sing these songs: "The Rose," page 117; "One Tin Soldier," page 279; "Try to Remember," page 301; "Erie Canal," page 258.

A short practice each day is better than a long practice once or twice a week. Patience and playing often will lead to a lifetime of enjoyment with the guitar.

CAN YOU READ THIS?

● **Can You Read This?**

You can read the words in a traffic sign because you have learned that certain letters represent certain sounds.

You can begin to read music as you learn which musical symbols represent which musical sounds.

Musical symbols can represent the rhythm of music. A series of notes that are the same represents an even rhythm pattern. For example, you can clap this steady quarter-note rhythm:

Combining symbols for longer and shorter sounds will make a more interesting rhythm. Clap this pattern:

Clap this more complicated rhythm pattern:

All of the patterns in "Can You Read This?" can be performed with a song in your book.

Add the musical staff and you can read the direction of the melody, up and down, along with the rhythm.

This simple *ostinato* melody moves up and then down. It always moves by *step*. Each note is just next door to the note before it.

This ostinato moves by *leap*. A leap jumps over the note next to it and moves to one that is further away.

This melody has an interesting pattern with a *dotted note*. Clap the ♪ pattern in groups of six:

$\frac{6}{8}$ meter also falls into a pattern of two. Each *measure* will have two dotted quarter notes. Clap the even pattern of two ♩..

Clap the even pattern of dotted quarter notes:

Take the dots off the quarter notes, and add an eighth note:

This melody uses all three of these $\frac{6}{8}$ meter patterns. The melody moves mostly by step.

Here is a longer melody. It will be easier to sing if you look for
repeated patterns.

Here are two melodies that can be sung with the same song. The
first one is quite simple.

Now try this more complicated melody. There are patterns that
repeat on different pitches. These repeating patterns are called
sequences.

Here are two melodies in minor tonality.

This melody will work with a song in your book. Be careful to observe the repeat pattern, or it will not fit!

repeat all
as needed

Sometimes this melody moves by step, and sometimes it leaps. The patterns are sometimes similar, but no two patterns are exactly alike. Patterns that are identical are easier to sing. However, variations in the pattern make the music more interesting.

Here is a melody in a major key. It begins with easy, even step-wise patterns, and then changes to skips and dotted patterns. Notice the meter changes!

THE SOUND BANK

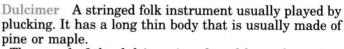

Bass Drum   A large, cylinder-shaped, metal drum with two "heads" made of stretched calfskin or plastic. The drum rests on its metal side and the player stands behind it, beating either side with a large, padded mallet.
• The bass drum is often used for dramatic effect in the orchestra. It can produce a deep booming roar or a soft, thudding heartbeat. *(p. 141)*

Chimes   A set of eighteen long, metal tubes (usually brass), suspended from a tall frame. The player stands beside them and strikes the top of the tubes with a wooden hammer.
• Chimes ring with a hollow, metallic tone and are frequently used to imitate church bells. *(p. 140)*

Clarinet   A cylinder-shaped wind instrument, usually wooden but sometimes metal or synthetic, with a single reed in the mouthpiece. The player blows into the mouthpiece to make the sound and changes the pitch by pressing keys on the body of the instrument.
• The clarinet has three "voices." In the lower register it is soft and hollow-sounding. The middle register is clear and bright, and the highest notes are more intense and can be very piercing. *(p. 17)*

Cymbals   Two shallow, metal plates, usually made of brass, fitted with leather hand-straps. One is held in each hand and they are clapped together to produce the sound.
• Cymbals vary in size. While large ones make an earth-shattering crash, small cymbals may be played for a light, delicate, rhythmic accompaniment. *(pp. 140, 202)*

Dulcimer   A stringed folk instrument usually played by plucking. It has a long thin body that is usually made of pine or maple.
• The sound of the dulcimer is soft and has a haunting, "faraway" quality. *(p. 184)*

English Horn   A wooden instrument shaped like a cylinder with a bulb-shaped bell at the bottom. It has a double reed that the player blows into to make the sound. Keys on the body of the instrument are pressed to change the pitch.
• The sound of the English horn is similar to the exotic "oriental" tone color of the oboe, but its "voice" is lower and the tone is richer and warmer. *(p. 138)*

Flute A small metal instrument shaped like a round piece of pipe. The player blows across an open mouthpiece in the side of the flute near one end, and presses button-like keys to change pitches. Originally flutes were made of wood, but most are now metal, some even gold or silver.
• The sound of the flute is pure, clear, and sweet. The lower notes are very soft and gentle; the higher register is brighter and louder. *(p. 62)*

French Horn A medium-sized brass instrument made of coiled tubing, with a large bell at the end. The player sits with the horn held down near the lap, and keeps one hand in the bell to control the pitch and tone. The lips *buzz* against the mouthpiece to make the sound. The pitch is changed by pressing valves on the side of the horn.
• The sound of the French horn is mellow and warm, and not as loud or assertive as the other brass instruments. *(p. 141)*

Gong A broad, concave metal disc, usually made of brass and hung vertically in a frame. The player strikes the gong slightly off-center with a soft-headed mallet.
• A sensitive player can evoke loud or soft, short or long tones from the gong, which reverberate with a rich, shimmering sound. *(p. 140)*

Guitar (acoustic) A wooden string instrument with six strings. The player strums or plucks it with a pick or the fingers to play a melody or chords.
• When played softly, the guitar is gentle and sweet. It sounds lush and full when it is played more loudly. *(p. 194)*

Guitar (electric) Electric guitars are flatter and usually made of plastic. They must be plugged into an amplifier.
• Electric guitars are much louder than acoustic guitars. They can make many special sounds with the help of electronics. *(p. 29)*

Oboe A small, wooden, cylinder-shaped wind instrument. The player blows into a double reed to make the sound, and changes pitch by pressing keys on the body of the instrument.
• The sound of the oboe is thin and sweet, often sounding exotic or melancholy. Unlike many other woodwind instruments, the sound gets sweeter and softer as it goes higher. *(p. 141)*

Recorder A simple wooden flute dating back to the Middle Ages. It is sounded by blowing into a "whistle" mouthpiece at one end. Holes on the body of the recorder are covered and uncovered to change the pitches.
• The recorder has a delicate, quiet tone, even in its more piercing higher register. The recorder comes in many sizes, the larger ones sounding lower, the smaller ones higher. *(p. 134)*

Saxophone A woodwind instrument invented by Adolphe Sax in the nineteenth century by placing a clarinet-type reed mouthpiece on a piece of brass tubing.
• The saxophone has a warm, brassy-but-mellow sound that makes it ideal in jazz ensembles. *(p. 17)*

Snare Drum A small, cylinder-shaped drum. Two heads made of calfskin or plastic are stretched over the metal shell and strings wrapped in wire ("snares") are fixed to the bottom. When the player strikes the top with sticks, the snares vibrate in response.
• A sharp, steady, rhythmic accompaniment is often played on the snare drum. It can also produce a long, raspy, rolling sound. *(p. 140)*

String Bass A large wooden string instrument that is either bowed or plucked. The string bass is taller than most players, who must stand up or sit on a tall stool to play it.
• The sound of the string bass is very dark and resonant, particularly in the lower notes. The plucked notes are very useful for establishing a strong "beat," both in classical music and popular music. *(p. 17)*

Tambourine A small, shallow drum with one head and a wooden shell. Circular metal disks ("jingles") hang loosely in pairs around the circumference of the shell. The player holds the tambourine in one hand and shakes it or strikes it with the other hand or on the hip.
• A shimmery, metallic sound rattles from the tambourine. *(p. 141)*

Timpani A set of two or more large, basin-shaped drums made of copper or brass, with calfskin or plastic stretched over the top. Each drum has a different pitch, which can be adjusted by means of a pedal at the base. Usually only one player is in charge of all the drums and plays them by striking the top with one or two mallets.
• The timpani are the most important percussion instruments, for they provide strong rhythmic and tonal support for the orchestra. They usually produce a deep, insistent rumbling but can also punch out sharp, loud notes. *(p. 23)*

Trombone A fairly large brass instrument with a large bell at the end of the tubing. The sound is made by *buzzing* the lips against the mouthpiece. The pitches are changed by pushing and pulling a metal "slide," lengthening and shortening the tubing.
• The trombone can sound very aggressive and noisy; but in its softer "voice" it can be warm and mellow. *(p. 202)*

Vibraphone A xylophone-like instrument with metal bars. An electronic device creates a slow or fast vibrato, giving the instrument its name.
• The vibraphone has a mellow, "sweet" sound, especially when the vibrato device is engaged. *(p. 17)*

Xylophone A pitched percussion instrument with a keyboard of wooden bars and played with mallets.
• The xylophone has a bright, brittle sound that makes it effective in percussive or humorous passages. *(p. 80)*

GLOSSARY

a cappella *(p. 72)* A term used to indicate unaccompanied choral singing; "in chapel style."

accent *(p. 116)* A single tone or chord louder than those around it (>).

acoustical (acoustics) *(p. 146)* Pertaining to the physical properties of sound: frequency (pitch), amplitude (loudness), overtone structure (tone color), and duration (length).

aria *(p. 43)* In an opera, oratorio, or a cantata, an extended song for solo voice; often a showpiece for the singer's vocal ability.

ballad *(p. 30)* A popular song that usually tells a story.

ballet *(p. 64)* A theatrical production centered on dance, generally with costumes, scenery, and accompanying music; or the music written for such a production.

bar line *(p. 116)* The vertical line on the staff, used to mark off groupings of beats.

beat *(p. 10)* A repeating pulse that can be felt in some music.

chorale *(p. 29)* A homophonic harmonization of a hymn tune. *See* homophonic texture.

chord *(p. 18)* Three or more different tones played or sung together.

(p. 188) A large group of singers.

Classic period *(p. 38)* The period encompassing the latter half of the eighteenth century and the early nineteenth century, when the style of composition was generally marked by simplicity, balance, and restraint.

coda *(p. 134)* A short closing section added at the end of a composition.

compound meter *(p. 153)* A grouping of beats in which three beats are felt as one.

concerto *(p. 25)* A piece for a solo instrument with orchestra, usually in three movements.

countermelody *(p. 132)* A melody that is played or sung at the same time as the main melody.

cross-rhythm *(p. 155)* A rhythm in which the regular pattern of accents is altered to form a new pattern.

diction *(p. 83)* The pronunciation and enunciation of words in singing.

dissonance (dissonant) *(p. 36)* An interval or a chord that sounds unstable, and pulls towards a consonance.

downbeat *(p. 155)* The first, usually accented, beat of the measure.

duet *(p. 185)* Any two-part composition written for two performers.

dynamic level *(p. 149)* The degree of loudness and softness.

ensemble *(p. 15)* A group of players or singers.

fanfare *(p. 163)* A tune for one or more brass instruments, usually short and made of strong, accented passages.

finale *(p. 64)* [fee NAH leh] Last movement of a composition, such as a symphony or concerto.

folk song *(p. 30)* A song of unknown authorship that has for generations been current among the people of a nation or region.

form *(p. 172)* The structure of a composition; the way its musical materials are organized.

fret *(p. 101)* A strip of metal across the fingerboard of a guitar or similar instrument. The player raises or lowers the pitch by pressing a string into contact with a fret.

fugue *(p. 133)* A musical form based on imitation, in which the main melody (subject) and related melodies (countersubjects) are varied in different ways. The texture is polyphonic. *See* polyphonic texture.

grand staff *(p. 79)* A two-staff system with the soprano and alto parts shown in the treble clef and the tenor and baritone parts shown in the bass clef.

graphic notation *(p. 57)* Notation using pictures to represent sounds (rather than using traditional notation for exact pitches.)

Gregorian chant *(p. 70)* *See* plainsong.

harmony *(p. 25)* A related succession of chords.

homophonic texture (homophony) *(p. 79)* A melodic line supported by a harmonic accompaniment.

improvisation *(p. 17)* The art of making up the music as the performer goes along.

interval *(p. 108)* The distance from one tone to another. The smallest interval in traditional Western music is the half step (f-f♯, f♯-g, etc.).

Contemporary music often uses smaller intervals, as does music of other cultures.

instrumentation *(p. 194)* *See* orchestration.

inversion *(p. 168)* Reversing the pitch direction of the tones of a melody.

jazz *(p. 16)* A style that grew out of the music of African Americans, then took many different substyles: ragtime, blues, cool jazz, swing, bebop, rock, etc. It features solo improvisations over a set harmonic progression.

key *(p. 42)* The particular scale on which a piece of music or a section of it is based, named for its tonic or key-tone or "home-base" tone. (The key of D major indicates that the major scale starting and ending on the tone D is being used.)

key signature *(p. 103)* An indication of key consisting of sharps or flats placed on the staff at the beginning of a composition.

major *(p. 102)* Tonally, a key that is based on a major scale—a scale that contains a step-pattern of whole, whole, half, whole, whole, whole, half.

measure *(p. 19)* A grouping of beats set off by bar lines.

medley *(p. 30)* A set of songs grouped together and sung without interruption.

melody *(p. 25)* A succession of single tones with rhythm, forming a recognizable musical idea.

meter *(p. 116)* The way beats of music are grouped, often in sets of two or in sets of three. The meter signature, or time signature (e.g., $\frac{3}{4}$, $\frac{2}{4}$), tells how many beats are in the group, or measure (top number), and the kind of note that gets one beat (bottom number).

metronome *(p. 129)* A mechanical or electronic device that indicates precise tempo markings.

minimalism *(p. 199)* A twentieth-century style of composition that emphasizes extended repetition of a motive or group of motives.

minor *(p. 104)* Tonally, a key that is based on a minor scale—a scale that contains a step-pattern of whole, half, whole, whole, half, whole, whole.

monophonic texture (monophony) *(p. 73)* A single unaccompanied melody line.

motive *(p. 111)* A short musical fragment.

movement *(p. 25)* Each of the smaller, self-contained sections (usually three or four) that together make up a symphony, concerto, string quartet, and so on.

multimeter *(p. 120)* Changing from one meter to another in successive measures.

neume *(p. 70)* Plainchant notation—originally slanted lines indicating the rise and fall of the melody. Later, various-shaped noteheads that rested on a four- or five-line staff.

notation *(p. 70)* Symbols that represent specific pitches and durations in music.

octave *(p. 108)* The distance of eight steps from one tone to another that has the same letter name.

opera *(p. 43)* A theatrical production combining drama, vocal and orchestral music, costumes, scenery, and sometimes dance.

oratorio *(p. 82)* A musical drama for voices and orchestra, often based on a religious narrative; usually performed without scenery or action.

orchestration *(p. 149)* The use of individual instruments and groups of instruments in writing or arranging a composition for an ensemble.

ostinato *(p. 18)* A musical idea that repeats throughout a piece or a section of a piece.

pentatonic *(p. 106)* Music based on a five-tone scale. A common pentatonic scale corresponds to tones 1, 2, 3, 5, and 6 of the major scale.

phrase *(p. 41)* A melodic idea that acts as a complete thought, something like a sentence.

pitch *(p. 14)* The highness or lowness of a tone.

plainchant *(p. 70)* *See* plainsong.

plainsong *(p. 70)* Monophonic chant sung usually with even rhythm on Latin texts. Plainsong is one of the earliest examples of notated music. *See* monophonic texture.

polyphonic texture (polyphony) *(p. 73)* Two or more independent melody lines sounding together.

polyrhythm *(p. 15)* Several different rhythm patterns going on at the same time, often resulting in conflicts of meter.

quartet *(p. 187)* Any four-part composition written for four performers.

reprise *(p. 245)* An abbreviated repetition of a song performed earlier.

retrograde *(p. 168)* A melody, or motive, read backward.

rhythm *(p. 10)* The combination of sounds and silences in the same or differing lengths.

rhythm complex *(p. 10)* A percussion composition consisting of layers of contrasting rhythm patterns. *See* polyrhythm.

riff *(p. 18)* A term used in jazz for a repeated, short, strongly rhythmic phrase. *See* ostinato.

Romantic period *(p. 52)* That period in the nineteenth century, following the Classic period, when the style of composition was generally marked by lyricism, fantasy, and emotional expression.

rondo *(p. 174)* A form in which the A section alternates with two contrasting sections, creating a plan of ABACA.

round *(p. 50)* A form in which a melody begins in one part and then is continually and exactly repeated by other parts in an overlapping fashion.

scale *(p. 42)* An arrangement of pitches from lower to higher according to a specific pattern of intervals. Major, minor, pentatonic, whole-tone, and chromatic are five kinds of scales. Each one has its own arrangement of pitches.

scat singing *(p. 56)* A jazz vocal style in which syllables are used instead of words.

score *(p. 67)* The musical notation of a composition, showing all vocal and instrumental parts.

sequence *(p. 111)* The repetition of a melody pattern at a higher or lower pitch level.

solo *(p. 185)* Music for a single performer, often with an accompaniment.

sprechstimme *(p. 56)* A vocal style somewhere between singing and speaking, used mainly by composers of atonal music.

staff *(p. 42)* A set of five equally spaced horizontal lines on which musical notes are written.

style *(p. 24)* In music, style refers to the way in which melody, rhythm, and harmony create a special "sound."

suite *(p. 69)* Any instrumental work of several short movements, often programmatic or descriptive.

symphony *(p. 60)* A large orchestral composition, generally in three or four contrasting movements.

syncopation *(p. 20)* An arrangement of rhythm in which prominent or important tones begin on weak beats or weak parts of beats, giving a catchy, "off-balance" movement to the music.

tempo *(p. 128)* The speed of the beat.

texture *See* homophonic texture, monophonic texture, polyphonic texture. ("Texture" may also refer to aspects of tone color and orchestration.)

theme *(p. 22)* An important melody that occurs several times in a piece of music.

tone cluster *(p. 66)* A group of tones lying no more than a step apart and produced, often on the piano, by pressing down on a section of the keyboard with the fist, forearm, or a board.

tone color *(p. 136)* The special sound of an instrument or voice.

transpose *(p. 168)* To write or perform music at a pitch other than the original one.

triad *(p. 42)* A chord of three tones, usually built in thirds—an interval of a third on top of another interval of a third.

trio *(p. 185)* Any three-part composition written for three performers.

triplet *(p. 124)* A rhythm pattern made by playing three equal sounds in the space of two of the same value.

unison *(p. 70)* The simultaneous playing or singing of the same notes by two or more performers, either at the same pitch or in octaves.

variation *(p. 112)* Music that changes a theme in some important ways.

vibrato *(p. 57)* A slight, rapid variation of pitch used to heighten the expressiveness of a tone.

vocal *(p. 56)* Any music or sound that is produced by the voice.

wave forms *(p. 68)* Basic electronic tone colors produced by an oscillator. Each waveform has a name that describes the way it looks when seen on an oscilloscope.

Classified Index

ENSEMBLES/INSTRUMENTALS

Beating the Blahs *190*
Fugue in G *134*
Glee Reigns in Galilee *202*
I'm an Old Cowhand *127*
Mangwani Mpulele *272*
Manipulations *168*
Rhythm Complex *10*
See Sharp *57*

FOLK AND TRADITIONAL SONGS

AFRICA
Mangwani Mpulele *272*
Tina Singu *301*

AFRICAN AMERICAN
He's Got the Whole World in His Hands *263*
Nine Hundred Miles *7*
On My Journey *170*
This Old Hammer *148*
When the Saints Go Marching In *196*

AMERICAN INDIAN
Wi Yo He Yo *303*

BRITISH ISLES
Hunter, The *78*
King of Love My Shepherd Is, The *79*
Men of Harlech *95*
Merry Minstrels *103*
Oh, Dear! What Can the Matter Be? *11*
We're All Together Again *80*

CHILE
Mi caballo blanco *118*
My White Horse *118*

CUBA
Elegua *13*

HISPANIC
Con el vito (Spain) *154*
De colores (Mexico) *130*
Elegua (Cuba) *13*
Laredo (Mexico) *186*
Mi caballo blanco *118*
My White Horse *118*

ISRAEL, HEBREW, JEWISH
Dodi Li *175*
Gilu Hagalilim *200, 201, 202*
Glee Reigns in Galilee *200, 201, 202*
Hatikvah *104*
Raisins and Almonds *281*
Tumbalalaika (arrangement) *120*

JAPAN
Sakura *282*

MEXICO
De colores *130*
Laredo *186*

SPAIN
Con el vito *154*

UNITED STATES
Erie Canal *258*
He's Got the Whole World in His Hands *263*
I Love the Mountains *269*
I Ride an Old Paint (medley) *30*
Mermaid, The *275*
Nine Hundred Miles *7*
Old Hundred *72*
On My Journey *170*
Puttin' On the Style *280*
Red River Valley (medley) *30*
Row, Row, Row Your Boat *113*
Streets of Laredo (medley) *30*
This Old Hammer *148*
When the Saints Go Marching In *196*

WEST INDIES
Hosanna *264*
Mary Ann *275*
Water Come a Me Eye *84*

HOLIDAY, SEASONAL, AND SPECIAL-OCCASION SONGS

PATRIOTIC
America *257*
America, the Beautiful *166*
Chester *34*
I Like It Here *265*
Marine's Hymn, The *99, 173*
Star-Spangled Banner, The *292*
This Land Is Your Land *114*

SPRING
De colores *130*
Sakura *282*
Spring Song *291*
While Strolling Through the Park *81*

THANKSGIVING
America *257*
America, the Beautiful *166*
King of Love My Shepherd Is, The *79*
Old Hundred *72*
Thanksgiving Calypso *298*

VALENTINE'S DAY
Hello, My Baby *100*
If *270*
Let It Snow *204*
Tell Me Why *132*
Where Is Love? *222*
You Are My Sunshine *21*
You've Got a Friend *304*

WINTER HOLIDAYS
Here We Come A-Singing   *260*
Jolly Old Saint Nicholas   *271*
Let It Snow   *204*
So My Sheep May Safely Graze   *290*

LISTENING LIBRARY

The following selections are heard in their
   entirety.

African-American Spiritual: *Swing Low, Sweet
   Chariot*   187
Alford: *Colonel Bogey March*   174
Anderson: *Belle of the Ball*   118
Applegate: *Coney Island Baby*   189
Bach: *Fugue in D Minor*   133
Bach: *Minuet*   170
Barber: *Adagio for Strings*   140
Bart: *Oliver!* selections   216
Bartók: *Mikrokosmos,* "Wrestling"   66
Beethoven: *Egmont Overture (Call Chart 4)*   51
Beethoven: *Für Elise (Call Chart 8)*   175
Beethoven: *Minuet in G*   66
Britten: *Young Person's Guide to the Orchestra,*
   "Introduction" *(Call Chart 9)*   207
Brooks/Vogel: *Some of These Days*   56
Brubeck: *Unsquare Dance*   157
Cage: *Dance*   59
Carter: *Etudes for Woodwind Quartet,* No. 3
   66
Ciani: *Composition for Synthesizer*   164
Davis: *You Are My Sunshine* (jazz version)   21
Eddleman: *Autoharp Fantasy*   59
Eddleman: *Brass Quartet* "In Honorem Paul
   Hindemith," Movement 1   140
Eddleman: *Tales from the Latin Woods*   141
Eisman/Carr: *Do the Mambo*   145
Ellington: *Dooji-Wooji*   144
Faini: *Afro-Amero (Call Chart 2)*   23
Foster/Brubeck: *Camptown Races* (jazz
   arrangement)   198
Glass: *The Photographer,* "A Gentleman's
   Honor"   199
Glière: *Russian Sailor's Dance (Call Chart 7)*
   141
Goodman/Christian: *Seven Come Eleven (Call
   Chart 1)*   17
Goodman/Christian: *Seven Come Eleven*
   (without call numbers)   19
Gottschalk: *Pasquinade,* "Caprice"   125
Grieg: *Peer Gynt,* "In the Hall of the Mountain
   King"   149
Handel: *Judas Maccabaeus,* "Hallelujah, Amen"
   82
Haydn: *St. Anthony Chorale*   29
Holst: *The Planets,* "Mercury"   69
Joplin: *The Entertainer*   125
LeCaine: *Dripsody*   58

Lennon and McCartney: *The Long and
   Winding Road*   139
Lewis: *The Golden Striker,* "No Sun in Venice"
   197
Liszt: *Concert Etude No. 3 in D$^\flat$ Major* ("Un
   Sospiro")   52
Lotti: *Kyrie*   74
Massenet: *Le Cid,* "Aragonaise"   208
McDaniels: *River*   147
Milhaud: *La cheminée du Roi René,* Movement
   1   140
Mozart: *Symphony No. 40 in G Minor,*
   Movement 3   36
Oh, Dear! What Can the Matter Be? (with
   rhythm complex)   12
Penderecki: *Threnody for the Victims of
   Hiroshima*   67
Peraza: *Gitano*   13
Plainsong: *Rex caeli, Domine*   73
Prince/Raye: *Boogie-Woogie Bugle Boy*   186
Prokofiev: *Classical Symphony,* Movement 3,
   "Gavotte"   60
Raaijmakers: *Contrasts,* Part 2 *(Call Chart 5)*
   69
Read: *The Aztec Gods,* Movement 1   140
Santana: *Gitano*   13
Schoenberg: *Pierrot lunaire,* "The Dandy"   56
Seeger: *Where Have All the Flowers Gone?*   29
Shostakovich: *Symphony No. 1 in F,* Movement
   2   36
Smaldone: *Piece for Synthesizer*   146
Sondheim: *Send In the Clowns* (two
   performances)   138
Sousa: *Washington Post March*   173
Steel Drum Band: *El Merecumbe*   193
Stravinsky: *The Firebird,* "Finale"   163
Traditional American: *Joe Turner Blues*   160
Traditional American: *Johnny Has Gone for a
   Soldier*   184
Traditional American: *When the Saints Go
   Marching In*   197
Traditional Mexican: *Cielito lindo*   194
Traditional Scottish: *Bagpipe Music*   195
Turner, et al: *Soulville*   14
Villa-Lobos: *The Little Train of the Caipira*
   129
Wagner: *Die Walküre,* "Winterstürme"   139
Zulu Folk Song: *Mangwani Mpulele*   155

POEMS AND LYRICS

Noise (Pope)   136
River (McDaniels)   147

THEME MUSICAL

Don't Go Anywhere Without a Song   210
Everything's Coming Up Roses   214
I Like Me   213
Never Say Never   215

Song Index

12	8	All for the Best *254*
12	8	America *257*
9	6	America, the Beautiful *166*
12	8	As Long As He Needs Me *(Oliver!)* *234*
9	6	By the Waters of Babylon *171*
5	4	California, Here I Come *111*
2	1	Chester *34*
8	6	Con el vito *154*
10	7	Coney Island Baby *188*
12	8	Consider Yourself *(Oliver!)* *225*
8	5	Dancin' *150*
6	4	De colores *130*
4	3	Dedication *83*
10	6	Dodi Li *175*
12	8	Dona nobis pacem *257*
11	7	Don't Go Anywhere Without a Song *210*
1	1	Elegua *13*
12	8	Erie Canal *258*
11	7	Everything's Coming Up Roses *214*
4	3	Fiddler, The *85*
11	8	Food, Glorious Food *(Oliver!)* *217*
12	8	Gaudeamus omnes in Domino *259*
11	7	Gilu Hagalilim *200, 201, 202*
11	7	Glee Reigns in Galilee *200, 201, 202*
5	3	Hatikvah *104*
5	3	Hello, My Baby *100*
12	8	He's Got the Whole World in His Hands *263*
12	8	Here We Come A-Singing *260*
6	4	Home on the Rolling Sea, A *133*
12	8	Hosanna *264*
3	2	How Troubled the Waters *53*
4	3	Hunter, The *78*
12	8	I Like It Here *265*
11	7	I Like Me *213*
12	8	I Love Pasta *266*
13	8	I Love the Mountains *269*
2	1	I Ride an Old Paint (medley) *30*
12	8	I'd Do Anything *(Oliver!)* *230*
5	3	I'd Like to Teach the World to Sing *107*
13	8	If *270*
9	6	If I Were You *171*
6	4	I'm an Old Cowhand *126*
2	2	In the Army *44*
9	6	It's Not So Easy Bein' Me *160*
1	1	Ja-Da *6*
13	8	Jolly Old Saint Nicholas *271*
5	3	Just in Time *110*

4	3	King of Love My Shepherd Is, The *79*
4	3	Kyrie *74*
10	7	Laredo *186*
11	7	Let It Snow *204*
13	8	Mangwani Mpulele *272*
5	3	Marine's Hymn, The *99, 173*
13	8	Mary Ann *275*
4	3	Men of Harlech *95*
13	8	Mermaid, The *275*
5	3	Merry Minstrels *103*
2	2	Metronome, The *50*
5	4	Mi caballo blanco *118*
13	8	Mighty Fortress Is Our God, A *276*
5	4	My White Horse *118*
11	7	Never Say Never *215*
1	1	Nine Hundred Miles *7*
13	9	Noble Dame *278*
2	1	NonChester *35*
6	4	Ode to Joy *135*
1	1	Oh Dear! What Can the Matter Be? *11*
8	5	Oh, Susanna *(arrangement in 7)* *151*
5	3	Old Abram Brown *99*
4	3	Old Hundred *72*
9	6	On My Journey *170*
5	3	One of Those Songs *97*
13	9	One Tin Soldier *279*
13	9	Puttin' On the Style *280*
13	9	Raisins and Almonds *281*
2	1	Red River Valley (medley) *30*
12	8	Reviewing the Situation *(Oliver!)* *240*
8	5	River *(lyrics only)* *147*
9	6	Rock Around the Clock *158*
5	4	Rose, The *117*
5	4	Row, Row, Row Your Boat *113*
13	9	Rozhinkes mit Mandlen *281*
13	9	Sakura *282*
8	5	Scatterbox *142*
13	9	Scattin' with Solfege *285*
13	9	Sentimental Journey *289*
1	1	Sing *5*
13	9	So My Sheep May Safely Graze *290*
2	1	Songs of the West (medley) *30*
13	9	Spring Song *291*
14	9	Star-Spangled Banner, The *292*
14	9	Step to the Rear *293*
2	1	Streets of Laredo (medley) *30*
6	4	Tell Me Why *132*
14	9	Thanksgiving Calypso *298*
5	4	This Land Is Your Land *114*
8	5	This Old Hammer *148*

9	6	Those Magic Changes	*161*
14	9	Time in a Bottle	*300*
14	9	Tina Singu	*301*
14	9	Try to Remember	*301*
5	4	Tumbalalaika	*120*
4	3	Water Come a Me Eye	*84*
4	3	We're All Together Again	*80*
10	7	When the Saints Go Marching In *196*	

2	1	Where Have All the Flowers Gone?	*28*
11	8	Where Is Love? *(Oliver!)*	*222*
4	3	While Strolling Through the Park	*81*
12	8	Who Will Buy? *(Oliver!)*	*236*
14	9	Wi Yo He Yo	*303*
2	1	You Are My Sunshine	*21*
5	3	You're Never Fully Dressed Without a Smile *109*	
14	9	You've Got a Friend	*304*

PICTURE CREDITS